SLEEP ON IT!

The Practical Side of Dreaming

by
Janice Baylis

DeVorss & Company
1046 Princeton Drive
Marina del Rey, California 90291

ISBN: 0-87516-234-7
Library of Congress Catalog Card Number: 77-74164

Printed in the United States of America
by Book Graphics, Inc.

Contents

Foreword

One thing is too certain; if we
insist on having hard ground under
foot all the way, we shall not get far.
                                    — Swinburne

Recently, progressive psychologists have begun to advocate dream study for average, normal people without the dependence on a trained psychologist. It is encouraging for people to hear this from the professionals. However, I think people will believe it, and act on it more, if they come in touch with experiences of people who have learned to use dreams without the aid of a psychologist. That is why I wrote this book.

Another reason for writing this book was to incorporate, eclectically the many purposes of dreams and the many approaches to understanding dreams. Due to the personality development emphasis of psychology, other dream books dwell almost exclusively on this area of dream guidance. Here we are turned to the neglected functions of dreams regarding daily matters of life.

These dreams illustrate the practicality of the dream voice in areas of health, occupation, finance, interpersonal relationships as well as your own character and spiritual development. You have a not-so-silent partner in the silence of sleep. Hopefully this book will prod you to form an active partnership with the subconscious levels of your mind.

The instructional approach is through examples. These examples were gathered while working in dream study groups of others like myself, average, non-psychologically trained people. For three years the groups were formed from interested members of A.R.E., Association for Research and Enlightenment. Of the many aspects of the life and work of the noted psychic, Edgar Cayce, these people were especially attracted to dream work.

Later, I began teaching adult education classes in dream interpretation. These classes drew people of all kinds from high school to late sixties; from doctors to housewives. In the book most of the names have been changed to protect the innocent, and the not so innocent.

Heraclitus once said, "To those who are awake, there is one world in common, but, of those who are asleep, each is withdrawn into a private world of his own." These private worlds are shared and explored with you. Use them as a guide to exploring and mapping your private inner world and relating yours to the 'one world in common'.

Janice Baylis
April 1977

Chapter One

Time to Wake Up

Why do we sleep? Why not get one-third more living done in our time on earth? Or have life over with one-third faster? We sleep to dream. We dream to wake us up to our selves:

Our instinctual self—body consciousness and survival drives.
Our directive self—images of life from childhood.
Our social self—personality and role-playing masks.
Our shadow self—'the Devil made me do it!', repressions.
Our balancing self—male, animus or female, anima.
Our collective self—archetypal images.
Our higher self—the Christ seed within, 'Know ye not that ye are Gods in the making!'

Three voices pounced on me as I entered the teacher's lounge.

"Come here, Jan, we need you!"

"Can you help me?"

"Mary's worried. I told her you'd said death in a dream usually means something else, but I can't tell what."

1

I turned to Mary, a very conscientious first year teacher. She worked very hard with her first graders. "Tell me the dream," I said.

Mary spoke. "I dreamed it was lunch time and the monitor brought the milk to the classroom."

I reasoned that the dream would either be about Mary's work or about a lesson she should learn. The setting of the dream was her school, her job setting. For non-teachers school settings in dreams usually mean the dream will present a lesson to the dreamer. Mary continued.

> The monitor brought the lunch milk. Bobby is on the milk list and usually eats at school but in the dream he was going home for lunch. After the children had all gone I noticed a carton of milk. I realized Bobby had forgotten to take it home with him. Then I picked it up and ran after him. I saw he had already crossed the street. I yelled at him and started across the street. I looked up and saw a car bearing down on me. As it knocked me down I knew I was going to die. I woke up terrified.

As I sat down beside Mary's box of homework papers and lesson plans, I said, "Is this the work you took home last night? What time did you leave school yesterday?"

She nodded, "Yes. I finally left at five-thirty. I stayed to get some things ready for Bobby. He needs so much extra help."

"That's it!" I said, "your dream is saying, 'You're knocking yourself dead' chasing after these kids! You'll 'knock yourself dead' if you try to be mother and teacher both."

"How true, how true," said Nancy. "We've all been telling you to take it easy. Didn't I say don't be such a mother hen?"

Everyone laughed, even Mary. "Thanks, Jan," she said. "That makes sense and I feel a lot better. I thought I was going to be run over by a car!"

"Dreams use emotionally packed, visual imagery to say the same things we would say with words," I explained.

"Don't people sometimes dream of coming death?" asked Sue.

"Yes," I said. "Sometimes they dream of it quite literally, especially if they aren't too afraid of dying. Abraham Lincoln dreamed:

> I hear weeping in the White House. I see a guard at the door of the East Room. I ask the guard what is wrong in the White House. The guard tells me that the president is dead, he has been shot by an assassin.

Lincoln had that dream about ten days before his death.

Last summer when my mother was dying I dreamed about it this way. You all knew Milton (a former teacher at this school who had died the previous spring from cancer). Remember how the treatments made him swell up so badly just before he died? Last summer when they sent my mother home from the hospital my sister left for Europe on vacation. I was due to go back east and visit my brother for the first time in twenty-five years. That would have left just my father here with Mother. Then I had this dream.

> I was going to see my sick mother. When I came in my Dad was seated behind her where she couldn't see him. He looked at me with despair and said, "Can you do something for her?" I realized he felt helpless. He just didn't know what to do. Then I noticed that my mother's legs were very, very swollen. (In reality she was very thin as she starved to death being unable to eat.) Seeing the swollen legs I got wet towels and put them on her legs. She smiled to show how good that felt. I was relieved that I had helped both Mom and Dad.

"When I woke up I realized the swollen legs were meant to remind me of the last person I knew who had died, Milton. Then, though she'd just been released from the hospital, I knew my mother was dying. I cancelled my trip. She soon took a turn for the worse. When the end came she was too weak to speak but she smiled as she passed away with her head in my hands. How thankful I was to have had that warning so my parents weren't alone at that sorrowful time."

"Wow," said Sue, "I guess dreams really do have meaning."

"Yes," I said, "Dreams can help us in so many ways!"

These incidents illustrate some basic principles of dream mechanics. Dreams picture common daily speech patterns as in 'knocking yourself dead'. Dreams may give a literal presentation as in Lincoln's dream prior to his own death. Symbolic reference appears in dreams as when the swollen legs stood for death. Commonly when a person dreams of death it stands for a rather large change. Something in their life is dying out, which is a natural step in growth cycles.

As my car pulled into the driveway I noticed my son's friend, Rob, sitting on the porch.

"Hi, Mrs. B., got any groceries you want me to help you with?"

"No, not today, Rob. You know Brian won't be home until about six-thirty," I answered.

"I know. It's you I came to see," replied Rob.

"Me?" I asked surprised.

"Yeah, Brian told me yesterday you're really into dreams and stuff like that. I'd like to ask you about a weird one I had some time ago. It was very vivid and it still bothers me."

"Sure, Rob," I said. "Go ahead."

> I was walking up a hill on a road. It was a bright sunshiny day. On the right it was nice and grassy, to the left was a ravine, rocky and weedy. A woman came down the road, gave me a flare and asked me to direct traffic. She said that there had been an accident ahead around a curve in the road. While I was walking back with the flare I saw something at the bottom of the ravine. Something compelled me to go down and see what it was. I thought maybe it was something thrown from the car in the accident. It was shadowy near the bottom as I got close but I was drawn on.

> When I got to it I saw it was the body of a
> younger Me, Dead! I looked at my dead self
> but I was not upset. It just felt eerie, the
> atmosphere was ghostly.

"What bothers me about that dream," said Rob, "is that I was dead and it didn't upset me. How come I wasn't scared or sad or something?"

"That's neat, Rob," I said. "Here you are rounding a bend in your road of life, between high school and now college; between childhood and adulthood. It was only your child self you saw that had died. The adult you can "send up a flare" and direct your traffic from now on. It is natural for childhood and the child self to die so the adult can live effectively. The sunshine was a good sign. And your reaction was good, you were not too emotional about it."

"Hey, that's great, Mrs. B. How did you get into this dream work anyway? You aren't a psychologist, I know that much."

"Everyone can learn to use their dreams, Rob, even modern psychologists say so."

For the reader's information, two psychologists, Calvin Hall and Vernon Nordby wrote a book, *The Individual and His Dreams*; in it they say, "There is no parallel to the kinds of self-knowledge a person acquires from the study of his dreams. It is a fascinating, rewarding task worthy of the strongest commitment." They also say, "Our aim is to take dreams out of the clinic and consulting room and demonstrate their value for enlarging everyone's understanding of himself and of the world in which he lives."

Another psychologist, Dr. Ann Faraday, put it this way in her book *Dream Power*. "There is absolutely no need for dream work to be restricted to special groups under the guidance of a psychologically trained leader. The kinds of techniques I have outlined can be used by anyone."

In answering Rob's question I went on to say, "But that isn't how I got started. You know Terry's mother next door, Mrs. Edwards. She and I started in an A.R.E. study group several years ago. That is when I began keeping a dream journal."

"What is A.R.E.? I've never heard of it," asked Rob.

"A.R.E. is the Association for Research and Enlightenment. It is based on the documented psychic readings of Edgar Cayce. He would go into a trance state and diagnose illnesses, give past life readings and sometimes he would interpret dreams people sent to him. In his recorded sessions people would ask questions too. He seemed to be answering from some level of Universal Consciousness. One time someone asked: "Give the best method of helping the human family increase in knowledge of the subconscious soul or spirit world."

He answered:

> Forget not that it has been said correctly that the Creator, the Gods and the God of the Universe, speak to man through this individual self. Man approaches the nearer condition of its approach to that field when the normal is at rest; sleep or slumber, and when more of the forces are taken into consideration, and are studied by the individual (not someone

else) it is the individual's job, each individual's
condition, each individual's position, each
individual's relation, each individual's mani-
festation, each individual's receiving the message from the higher forces themselves, and
for each individual to understand if they will
study, to show themselves approved.

Cayce Reading 3744-4

"There you have it. Both scientists and psychics
agree, dreams are one of our best sources of information about ourself, our World and our God."

"Is that all you do?" asked Rob, "just keep a journal
of your dreams?"

"Oh, no, I've taken college courses, A.R.E. classes,
psychology workshops and collected a lot of books on
the subject of dreams. But a person wouldn't have to go
into it so deeply. The real fun and understanding came
when I began working in dream-study groups. Just
average adults in A.R.E. or adult education groups, no
trained psychologists. I've been doing this for five years
now.

"If we were psychologists we might feel confined to
one approach. In our groups we are eclectic. We freely
apply any approach we want to. We don't have to be
Freudians or Jungians or Gestaltist or anything. What
we look for is that our dream meanings fit the life situation of the dreamer. It could relate to any aspect of
their life, sex, health, work, finances, interpersonal
relations, personality, spiritual insight or creativity.
We look at all sides."

"But gosh, Mrs. B., dreams are so weird. How can you understand what they mean? They seem so ridiculous," said Rob.

"I could write a whole book about that," I chuckled.

"Why don't you?" he suggested.

I replied, "I'd rather just write about the times I've seen dreams help people in their lives—very practical ways. Just to get people fascinated and develop their respect for the scope of the dreaming mind."

Rob agreed, "I've heard that we only use about one-tenth of our mind potential. Yet some people have ESP and telepathy and stuff like that."

"That's right," I answered. "Your mind is like an iceberg. By far the smaller part is visible or conscious, only about one eighth. Much of that notorious ninety percent unused mental capacity can be tapped by listening to your dreams. This means of tuning into our hidden mind resources is a safe and natural way.* No drugs needed.

"Speaking of telepathy, one night a friend of Mr. B.'s came over and they were talking when I went to bed. This man had gotten Dick into a business deal once and we'd lost quite a bit of money so I didn't like him. I dreamed he was trying to get Dick to invest in a deal in Riverside County. The next day I found out

---

*Scientific experiments in dream deprivation have been conducted at Maimondes Dream Laboratory. Sleepers connected to electronic devices were awakened every time they began to dream. They were allowed other levels of sleep but never the dream stage. After about five nights of dream deprivation they either dropped out of the test or began to suffer disorientation, hallucinations, anxiety or anger and grouchiness. When again allowed to dream, they had extra dream periods to catch up on what dream time they had lost.

that was exactly what they were talking about. I'd
picked it up by telepathy. (see chapter 3)

"Come here, Rob, I'll show you a demonstration I
use in my dream class I teach at adult education. I use
a dismantled wooden ladder from the pet shop.

"Here is one pole of the ladder. Visualize the conscious mind as a long pole. We use this pole to probe
the environment, gathering information through our
five senses. Then we use our rationality, logic and
emotions to judge and react. That's the way our waking
mind works. But we have other levels of mind," I said
as I picked up the other side of the wooden ladder.

"Visualize the unconscious mind as another pole,
which during sleep probes the world further through
ESP, discovering facts and relationships unseen by the
conscious reaches of our minds."

As I put the rungs between the poles of the ladder I
kept explaining. "Remembered, recorded and understood dreams can act as the rungs of a ladder to make
connections between these two levels of mind, conscious
and unconscious. When the two poles of mind are connected they become aligned. They can both be raised
and used as a ladder to climb to greater heights. From
the vantage points along the rungs (dreams) one gets a
broader more complete view of his life and the world."

"I see what you mean," said Rob. "But I still don't
see how you make sense from the silly things that happen in dreams."

"It takes time," I replied. "But after many examples
one begins to learn the language. If I ever write a book

that's the way it will be. Chapters of examples of practical guidance real people have experienced from their dreams. I'm keeping a file of these now, just in case. Hopefully, by surrounding a reader with a couple hundred examples he would begin to absorb and learn dream language kind of by osmosis. One could learn the language painlessly while enjoying some interesting stories."

"But can you give me any hints for right now, while I'm waiting for your book?" he asked.

"Well, yes," I said. "Why don't you come over tomorrow and I'll give you some ideas."

Dreams sometimes use sound, voice, smell, motion, etc. but mostly they use visual imagery. This means they find ways to make a picture of what we would say with words. Most of the symbol associations in dreams do have a kind of logic. Some concepts are not visible, such as thinking. Hair and thinking both come from our heads, but hair is visible and thinking is not. Dreams use hair to represent thinking.

Once when I was in a spell of depression and thinking dark, negative thoughts, I dreamed my hair was dyed black. It looked awful! I washed it in the dream and some of the black came out. Still I knew I would have to wash it several more times, before I'd get all of the black out. I needed to cleanse my thinking to get back to normal.

Sometimes the association is a little more remote. For example, Madeline dreamed:

> Gloria brought me an envelope with hair curlers in it. (What had Madeline been enveloped in?) They were some curlers I had used while visiting at Barbara's home. (Barbara is a mutual friend of Madeline and Gloria.) Gloria was bringing me back these curlers I had at Barbara's to curl my hair.

This dream came after Madeline had a talk with Gloria which showed her that Barbara had twisted her thinking. So much so, in fact, that it would "curl your hair"! The talk with Gloria helped Madeline straighten out her thinking and get rid of Barbara's kinky influence. The dream supports Gloria.

Slang expressions like "curl your hair" come up often in dreams, but usually referred to through pictures. You know the expression "the natives are restless" and that it means someone is pushing others too far so there is liable to be an uprising. This figure of speech is part of the next dream example which also uses proper names to show how words can have augmented meanings in dreams. It is a father's dream.

> I am in a jungle. I watch Tyrone *Power* and Gene *Tierney* acting in a movie. In the background is the ominous pound of native drums beating restlessly. I fear an uprising.

As a father he acted with absolute *power* and *tyranny*! The dream warned him that his teenaged children were about to rebel.

Another thing dreams do in using pictures is give us an object or word, then we have to change the spelling or break it into syllables. Even the ancients knew this. A good example is the dream which Alexander the Great had while he and his army were laying seige to the city of Tyre. Alexander dreamed he saw a satyr. His dream interpreter, Aristandros, divided the word, written from the picture seen, into two elements. *Sa* in Greek meant "your" and Tyre was the name of the Phoenician city then under seige. So, said Aristandros, the dream was telling Alexander 'the city of Tyre will be yours.' History shows that the dream was correctly precognitive.

Dreams are mainly commenting on the present life situation of the dreamer. To do this adequately may require a look at something from the past which is still an influence in the present. A forty year old Mexican-American woman with a serious marriage problem had this dream.

> Sylvia walked toward me. I noticed white things on her clothes. As we stood face to face, I saw that they were little white lice. They jumped off of her and on to me. I tried to pick them off but there were too many. I woke feeling squirmy and awful.

Sylvia was a new girl at the place where the dreamer worked. The only association the dreamer could come up with was that Sylvia was nineteen years old. I asked the dreamer what had happened to her when she was nineteen. The dreamer, our forty year old Mexican-American woman, stated that she was nineteen when she was married. Now we were getting someplace.

Many little "white lies" (lies in Spanish dialect sounds like lice) were put on her when she was a bride. Now she is facing them and trying to rid herself of them but it is very uncomfortable. Still, seeing them as little white lies and not malicious untruths was helpful.

This may seem like an arbitrary interpretation. But I remember when the dreamer experienced the insight it gave her. Her face lit up with what I call the "Ah ha!" of truth. It fitted her perfectly and she learned something! That is the test of a good interpretation no matter how arbitrary it may sound on paper.

Many dreams are retrocognitive, especially since childhood influences often remain very strong. But also many dreams are precognitive. Edgar Cayce stated that dreams prepare us on a soul level and therefore we dream every major happening of our lives before it happens. In my experience I have found dream precognition to be very common. However, it is often unrecognized because people don't keep records of dreams. Also they don't realize that the future event may be presented symbolically not literally.

Dream precognition varies greatly in degree both as to importance and as to the degree of symbolism. A woman whose marriage was in bad shape because of a difference of interests and leisure time activities, had this dream.

> I am in a Goodwill secondhand store. I am buying a dress. It is ivory colored and has sequins (sequence) on it. One seam is torn. A clerk recommends a seamstress who can mend it. There is a ticket on the dress

with a secret message. If you rub the ticket
with your fingernail the writing will appear. I do this and the ticket says
"Go Go
To To
Rio Rialto"
I know this is the name of the former dress
owner. It is her club name as a member of
a traveling club.

The second-hand store symbolizes a second chance
at goodwill. Not pure white but close to it. The torn
seam is the growing separation in her marriage. Something that seems stress (seamstress) can really be the
thing to fix the separation at this point in the sequence
(sequins) of the marriage. The secret is in membership
in a traveling club. Her husband often went on week-
end breakfast flights with a flying group. She would
never go and lately he didn't even ask. Two weeks later
he invited her to go on a breakfast flight to Rialto,
California, which is in Riverside County (Rio means
river). The message was clear—Go to Rialto! She did
and it was the beginning of many such weekend excur-
sions which she learned to enjoy. It brought much
goodwill to the marriage.

Early in my use of dreams for guidance and problem-
solving I had this dream encouraging me to use my
dream faculties.

I am in a school faculty meeting. We are
talking about how to teach problem-solving
to our students. One teacher says that she
wants to buy her son an extra fiddle so he
can practice fiddling with his friend. But

her boy wants wind-shield wipers for his car. (This shows a real desire to stop fiddling around and get a clearer view in stormy situations.)

Another teacher mentioned a book with the word *animal* in the title that was for teaching problem-solving. I said, "What is the gist of the method?" He said, "To just smile and say 'No problem, no problem'." I said, "That's what my husband does. When I have a problem and need help or want to talk about something he says 'No problem, no problem'. That makes me furious, just furious!"

Then the two teachers who were on my teaching team and myself began telling that we all keep dream journals. The rest of the faculty said that they did too. It turned out that Mrs. Henry, the teacher of the developmental primary class *for immature kids,* was the only teacher on the faculty that didn't keep a dream journal!

Hopefully, the examples in the following chapters will awaken many readers to these hidden faculties within themselves.

Chapter Two

Nightwatchman on Duty

Mr. Boozer woke up cussing, "Ouch, Damn it! Wake up, Honey, the ceiling's falling!"

"What's wrong?" his wife sat up in bed quickly. She gave him a shove and lay back down mumbling, "The sky isn't falling in, 'Chicken Little', you've been dreaming again."

"Humph, that must have been a dream, that plaster falling on my head. But my headache is just as real as if I'd been hit by plaster. Some dream!" said Mr. Boozer.

"Sure, what do you expect?" wife replied. "You were 'plastered' last night—as usual! Just like last week; remember you got 'stewed' Saturday night and then dreamed we had a huge stewed chicken hanging in our kitchen!"

"Yeah, I remember. In that dream I also knocked over the Scotch and had nothing left to drink but orange juice," he mumbled.

"Maybe, just maybe, your dreams are telling you to knock off the Scotch and the plastering and switch to decent stuff like fruit juice," answered his wife.

"Well, those dreams may think they're funny but this headache isn't," he mumbled. "I'll try to do better next week. This looks like another wasted 'hung-over' Sunday!"

> Late in 1974 Nadia Marech of Budapest, Hungary, kept having the same dream. She would wake up screaming in the middle of the night and tell her husband Jan, "I've had it again. A pale white hand is pointing at me and there are six fingers bunched together. Whatever can it mean?"
>
> The pregnant woman learned its meaning in January when her son Edouard was born. The baby had six fingers on each hand. Budapest doctors are more interested in her dreams than the child's extra digits. They are trying to understand the link between the malformation and her nightmares.*

Our unconscious mind is always aware of the cellular condition of our body and of where our health habits are taking us.

Obviously, what we take into our bodies—food, booze or otherwise—has a big effect on our health. In self-defense the body-consciousness sends us dreams of guidance about our diet.

A young woman had recently gone to work and acquired the coffee break habit. Her body objected to the nervousness created by too much caffein. Her dream:

*Reprinted by special permission from FATE Magazine, November 1976.

> I walked into my dining room (shows the area of concern is food intake). In the middle of the floor was a chicken brooder shaped like a very large coffee pot. On top the pot was smoking a cigarette. All of the baby chicks died. I felt sad about the dying chicks.

While recording the dream in her journal she could easily see the meaning. For her body coffee was bad, as bad as cigarettes for most people, she was a non-smoker. Coffee was killing the life, new cell growth, that should be hatching in her body.

While on vacation one gal dreamed:

> I'm at a table and in walks a pig in a dress. It is my pet pig and I think it is just darling. I am showing it to my visiting in-laws. I can hardly wait to take it home and show it to my children.
>
> Then I realize that it is just a baby pig now and that is why it is so cute. But if I keep it it will grow to be a big fat pig. I realize what a problem a big pig would be around home!

In other words, it is okay, within-the-law, to be a little piggy while on vacation. But it would become a big fat problem if continued at home!

If you are eating too much, or not enough, of something you will dream about it. If it is a real diet problem not being dealt with there will be a series of dreams. Some will tell what you're doing wrong and some will tell what to do about it. Here is a series of dreams all from the same dreamer. See if you can tell what they mean.

(1) I heard a radio announcer asking people to send in recipes for hamburger or cottage cheese innovations.

(2) I'm looking at a very, very long table of party food. A voice says, "You should quit where you long and long. Usually that's where you're wrong!" A hand gave me a lavender ticket good for twenty-five cents off on a double-deck hamburger at a nearby restaurant.

(3) I'm at the meat counter in the Lucky Market. I pick out four small pieces of steak, even though there are five in my family. (This is what I really do because I feel meat is too expensive for me, I eat just a bite or two off each piece.)

While the butcher is getting paper to wrap the four steaks he shows me a large piece. I think of the cost and say, "No thanks." He wraps the large steak and puts it in my cart anyway. My mother appears behind me and asks, "Why did you let him do that?" I say, "Well, I want to keep shopping here and I don't want him to be mad at me."

Would you say she needed to 'beef up' her diet with meat and protein? All that was needed to figure that out was to keep a dream journal and go back and read it. That is how to discover dreams in a series which will be scattered in between dreams about other topics.

Mothers often dream dietary advice for their children. One mother dreamed up a cottage cheese, apricot and walnut salad for her teen-aged daughter's lunch. In the dream she 'realized' it was because the apricots had lots of iron. This served to draw her attention to her daughter's increasing need for iron, due to the monthly loss of blood.

When Sir Christopher Wren was at Paris about 1671, he was ill and feverish, made but little water, and had a pain in his reins. He sent for a physician, who advised him to be let blood, thinking he had pleurisy: but bleeding much disagreed with his constitution, he would defer it a day longer: that night he dreamt, that he was in a place where palmtrees grew (suppose Aegypt), and that a woman in a romantic habit, reached him dates. The next day he sent for dates which cured him of the pain in his reins.

— Sir Christopher Wren 1632–1723
Architect*

Closely akin to booze and diet problems is the drug problem. One mother had this dream:

> My teen-age son had a high-boy chest in his bedroom. He moved it into our dining room. We were arguing about this when I woke up.

*From *Gates of Horn and Ivory: An Anthology of Dreams,* compiled by Brian Hill (Taplinger Publishing Company 1968). Copyright © 1967 by Brian Hill. Reprinted by permission.

She soon learned he had been getting 'high' on drugs. It had started in his private life (bedroom) but it became a family problem soon after this dream.

In this next case the mother and son were more fortunate. She caught the problem before the explosion. She had this dream two weeks after an argument had led her son to move into a friend's apartment.

> I saw my son's car parked between a couple of his friends' cars. (his body now rests with friends) Some kids had painted his car with black battery acid, it was about to explode. The kids were trying to get towels out of the car. I chased them away. Another kid ran back again. I grabbed him and said, "Get away from here you ass-head!" My husband appeared and scolded me for using such language with young people. I explained that I had to get his attention and get him away before the car exploded.

The expression ass-head was completely out of character for the dreamer. It sounds like acid and the car had been painted with black acid. She began to fear this son might be getting mixed up with LSD. She talked with him and learned that the other boy was using drugs and having parties at the apartment. Her son was trying not to get involved but it was hard. Since the dream said some other kids had painted the acid on his car, she believed him. They talked it over with the father and their boy came back home!

As the body is the vehicle carrying the soul through

life, a person's vehicle, car, or a child's bicycle, often appear in dreams to represent the body. One of my own dreams:

> I was riding in my car with a friend. She said, "Where is Chris?" I answered, "Chris is in the back seat."

Chris is, sounds like crisis. Two weeks later I was at the doctor's with a crisis in my backseat. I had a kidney infection!

However, not all dreams use symbols, some are pretty literal. I had had trouble with my car radiator. One night I dreamed my car began to steam just before I got on the ramp to enter the freeway. I took the precaution of having my son check the radiator. It was leaking! It pays to look at your dreams for the message that best fits your life situation.

Incubation is the practice of asking for dream guidance for problem solving. Dream incubation was practiced in nearly every ancient culture usually for physical healing. In the Greco-Roman world from the sixth century B.C. to the sixth century A.D. incubation was at its peak. Certain Greek temples were dedicated to Aesculapius, the God of healing. One such temple at Halike contains seventy case records telling the patient's name, disease and the dream that cured.

The patient or a friend would go to the temple and perform rites, to prime the subconscious. Then they would sleep there until they remembered a dream which was told to a trained interpreter stationed at the temple. Modern prayer before sleep often produces similar results.

Please do not take this to mean that I advocate giving up doctors and treating yourself. By no means is that the intent. Often the answer given will be to seek professional help. Here is such an example from my own life and dreams.

I had begun to have pains in my lower right side. First I went to a doctor to have it checked but he could find no cause. So, I decided to try the castor oil packs mentioned in the Edgar Cayce readings. This consists of flannel soaked in castor oil and applied to the aching area with a heating pad. After a couple of days of this I dreamed:

> There was a can of hot grease on my kitchen counter. I knocked it off and spilled it. As it came toward my bare right foot I pulled the foot back. The hot grease didn't hit me.

I figured that meant 'knock it off,' that is not a 'hit,' that is a misunderstanding (feet often mean understanding).

The next night I prayed. "I've been to the doctor. I've tried what I know of, but, I still hurt. Please tell me what I should do." A dream came after a couple of nights of prayer, call it suggestion if you like. Before I tell the dream a little more background is needed. Two years before this I was in an automobile accident. My car was hit from the rear and pushed into a car stopped in front of me. At the time I felt some pain in the upper back. That area was x-rayed and looked okay. The dream with the answer:

I was driving on a slow downgrade (my problem area was on the downgrade since the accident). The traffic was inching along. A small combination bolt and funnel shaped object kept popping out of a white cylinder which ran along the floor board of my car. Suddenly I realized my brakes had given out (the problem could no longer be stopped). I pulled out the pieces and the cylinder and put them on the hand truck which my car had become. There were three service stations nearby but the nearest one was a Mobil Station. I had a credit card for Mobil so I went there. The mechanic told me it would take five hours to fix my car and it would be finished at three A.M.

The boss of the station was behind the counter. He said dejectedly, "I'm a chiropractor. I guess I can't do anything. No one seems to want a chiropractor."

I felt very sorry for him and so I said, "Just because I need a mechanic now doesn't mean I won't need a chiropractor someday. Lots of people do."

"Oh, Good!" he cried. Then he pulled me over the counter which had become the backseat of my car. He began kissing and hugging me. I realized I'd have to smooch with this chiropractor, boss, until the mechanic had my car fixed. He then seemed sort of attractive after all.

I took the dream's advice and consulted a chiropractor. His full spinal column x-ray amazed me. I knew it was me because of certain missing teeth and fillings. Both the neck and lower spine were very curved. Evidently the bolt and funnel shaped pieces represented the vertebrae and the long floorboard cylinder was the spinal column. The five hours matched the number of treatments I needed, five. These were finished in the third month, March, probably related to three A.M. in the dream. At any rate I haven't had the pains in my lower right side since these mechanical adjustments were made!

Many people procrastinate when they need to *go in* to the doctor. Especially if they are afraid what the report will be. One such case prompted this dream:

> Mrs. Goin rang my doorbell. I opened the door and Mrs. Goin said, "My doctor has my case diagnosed. He knows because of my heavy breath."

This dream came to a woman who had previously had an operation for breast cancer. She had been in for some checkup x-rays but kept putting off going in for the report. When we discussed it we decided that Mrs. Goin was a perfect choice for the dream to use to bring her this important message. The real Mrs. Goin had just been told by her doctor that she quit work or he wouldn't be responsible for her health. This further frightened the dreamer. Goin spelled in syllables is go in!

The dreamer controlled her fears, symbolized by the heavy breath, and went in for the report. As it turned out she got a clean bill of health; felt much relieved and was so glad this dream led her to go in and get the good word.

Not all conditions need professional service, for example a coming common cold led to this basic advice.

> I dreamed a burglar was breaking into my bedroom. I crept out into the garden behind him and started throwing lemons from my tree. He ran back over the fence.

Another bit of common sense advice. A child told this dream to his mother, one of my dream students.

> I was captured by the Germans (germs). I was planning an escape. I had some pink chalk and I made marks I could follow later to get away from them.

A few days later when the boy was packing to go to summer camp, his mother made sure he took Pepto-Bismol tablets. These pink chalk-like tablets came in handy for the boy at camp. He got sick but he had the escape device ready!

People who aren't getting enough exercise can expect to dream about it. One 'hippy' friend who was developing middle-age spread reported this dream:

> An attractive man (men often mean action) was going to be conducting early morning exercises. He asked Katie, an athletic friend in the same age bracket, and myself to join. Katie chose a bright pink, long-legged sweat suit. I tried on some gray short sweat pants. These were size seven, my former size, they were too small. Someone tossed me a size nine, these fit better.
>
> I was still hesitating about joining. The

> instructor really wanted me to, so he offered to save me money by getting me a second-hand sweat suit. I wanted a bright color like yellow, orange or pink. Part of the routine would be cycling through the neighborhood.

The message—a program of exercise would suit the dreamer, in colors of vitality!

Another case in point, a teaching friend's dream giving her a physical education (P.E.) lesson.

> As part of my team teaching I was supposed to measure two classes of students for their P.E. records. The other teacher was lazy and had excused a lot of her kids from P.E. (the lazy side of the dreamer). My sister came around as an inspector, so I quickly got started. I took Dennis W., a very strong well-built student in my own class. I was measuring his chest expansion. I hoped the inspector wouldn't discover that so many of the lazy teacher's students weren't there for P.E. I felt worried.

For many years my husband's back slipped out of alignment at the slightest strain. Then he began doing 'jumping jack' exercises. He has had very little back problem since starting this routine. This exercising has been a real treasure to him. He often urged me to join in but I neglected to do so. After my chiropractic adjustments I had this dream.

> My husband is driving my car down the street talking to me about how to drive it.

> We see a new store, "The Treasury". He
> drives right into the carpeting department.
> (This treasure might help our sex life, pet-
> ting!) We leave my car to be washed. We
> go up on the escalator. I am looking at
> swimming suits then I am looking for a
> jumpsuit in women's wear. I didn't find
> any and then I couldn't find my husband.

He's telling me how to drive my car, that is, he has a
suggestion for me on how to direct my body. It is a
treasure. I should look for swimming and jumping.
Like the escalator, they would give me a lift.

Remember the teacher in chapter one who, due to
overwork, dreamed she was knocking herself dead
chasing after her students? Other people with low vitality have had similar dreams. Here's one. This dreamer
needs energy.

> I'm at the service station getting gas.
> Some robbers come and start to steal all
> the fuel.

Another from a teacher friend.

> I'm giving a test to my class (it is a testing
> situation). While I'm reading the answers
> from the answer sheet (the answer follows),
> I feel that I want to hide from the kids. I
> feel I need to get some sleep. I go to the
> front seat of my car. Then to hide I get
> down on the floor and put my head on the
> seat.

Once when I was feeling very tired but had work at
school I felt had to be done, I had this dream.

> Halfway to school my car ran out of gas
> (no energy). I pushed the car the rest of the
> way to work. When I walked into the
> teacher's workroom none of the regular
> teachers were there. Everyone else had
> called a substitute!

That morning when I woke up I decided, no one else
would push himself to work feeling like this. I called
a sub.

A mother, wife, nurse had the following dream
pointing up her need for more vitality.

> It began with a typical hassel getting my
> children off to school (the strains of moth-
> ering). Then I was walking with a girl. We
> came to an old frame house that was a kind
> of help station. The girl called it Two
> Roses Place (dreamer had two labors of
> love, her family and her nursing). The girl
> had two flags on sticks, one was faded
> green, the other very faded .yellow. She
> said, "Yellow for vitality, green for virility."
> She stuck the flags in the lawn. I said,
> "That yellow isn't very bright." She said,
> "I know, my yellow never is very bright."
> I was thinking "I've seen yellow much
> brighter than that and it is so much pret-
> tier!" I wanted very much to get a better
> flag for the lawn because I knew the house
> was a place that did good for people.

As this dream hints, sex, virility, is closely tied in with
one's vitality. Sex problems can be quite varied even
with normal people. The Freudian approach to sex in
dreams was extreme because he worked only with very

ill persons. Much sexual advice does come through our dreams depending on the individual situation.

The nurse took steps to improve her vitality and got the improved virility spin-off that was hinted at. She then dreamed.

> My husband had a flashy new car (his body is looking good to her). He also had a box for me, wrapped for mailing.

The box is a typical Freudian sex symbol for the female. Then if you change the spelling but not the sound of mailing to maleing, you can see the meaning.

This next dream with advice for a woman's sex life is a little complicated. Her personality was affecting her relationship to her husband. She had too much masculinity in the make-up of her personality.

Siblings of the same sex appearing in a dream often, not always, mean the dream indicates an alternative life style the dreamer could adopt. Her sister is with her in this dream. The opening of a dream usually presents the area of concern. In this case they are going to be in couples, the dream is about male/female relationships. Now the dream.

> My sister and I come out of a theater (dream says picture this way of acting). We are going to dinner with several couples (male/female). We go into the restroom to clean up. My hands are very dirty (as if she'd been doing man's work). I wash them. I also wash my face and start a complete make-up job (she should change her make-up, that is personality). I did my

eyebrows which I never do in reality (a strictly feminine touch).

I'm wearing a black lacy, sexy slip (her sex life was slipping). I look in a mirror (facing herself!). I see a bed with two young boys in it (it has been as if her husband was taking an immature boy to bed instead of a wife). I borrowed my sister's lipstick. It was very red-red and liquidy but it rubbed right off and barely left any color on me (menstruation, a sign of femininity, rubbed off her without coloring her personality). I found another lipstick, pink (color symbolic of love and femininity). It looked good on me.

I had a black lacy scarf to put over my hair (think sexy). I painted the edge of the scarf with pink from the lipstick (think love). It looked very pretty. My sister complimented me on my looks and my taste in clothes. We went out to meet our husbands. I was hoping he would make love to me later.

The opposite, too much sex, is the problem in this woman's marriage. She has recently married for the second time. They are still in the experimental stage of their road through life together,

My husband and I are in a strange car (cars often symbolize the way you are moving through life). It is an experimental model, long, low, red and very streamlined (phallic symbol). A hose of some kind breaks and squirts milky-white liquid in my face. It stings. The tube keeps overflowing

> and the liquid is filling the car. I ask my husband to pull over and stop the car so the tube of liquid can be fixed and we can clean up the mess in the car.

The excessive sexuality in her marriage hurts her, stings. She needs to face this stinging situation. She will have to talk to her husband about it, ask him to fix his sexuality and not make a mess of their life together.

Young unmarried people may think unlimited sexual freedom is okay, but their dreams indicate otherwise. They themselves, from the totality of their being, are making the judgement. This is the dream of a modern high school girl.

> I'm wearing just blue jeans (toplessness shows the feminine freedom concept). I'm sliding down an icy hill on my backside (back-sliding). In the background are people surrounding a ballpark, I'm sliding away from the people with my friend (she is not 'in the ballpark'). I slide down the icy hill a few times.
>
> At last the scene changes. I slide to an old shack ("shacking up"). It is dark now. There is a man going to spend the night there too. He is dressed in western style (a midnight cowboy!). The bathroom is shabby, it has a mirror on the wall (reflect on this). There comes a knock at the door. It was a fox-like creature but trying to disguise itself and hiding behind the screen door. It sticks its paw through a hole in the screen. I know he is hoping I'll fall for it and let him in. The fox is smiling slyly with

his big teeth showing. I am afraid of him
and his paw! I tell the man in the bathroom
that someone is at the door. He comes to
the door and looks pleased. He sees the
paw and smears vaseline on it. I was
shocked to see how he reacted to the fox,
no fear at all. The fox was pleased because
he was getting what he wanted. I am afraid.

She has a right to fear shacking up with sly foxes!
Only they get what they want, she would just be a loser.
Young men get similar messages. This is from a college
boy.

I'm in a shopping mall. (He has been
mauling, that is handling roughly, some of
the girls in his shopping around.) I walk
through the Toyota building and the
Broadway Store. (He'd been toying with
the 'broads'.) Then I realize I'm lost! I
don't know my way back to where I left my
car. I see a booth with my college counselor
in it. (The counselor is a friendly authority
figure.) He tells me the way back to my
car. On the way I pass a church and hear
beautiful hymns (hims).

If he would go back to his old ways of respecting
females he would be a beautiful him.

Even parents get in on the teen-age sex scene. This
was an alerting dream for the mother with a precognitive hint of the boy's nocturnal adventures with the
girl next door. The boy was only thirteen but was
sneaking out at night to meet the girl in the backyard
after their parents were asleep. The mother's dream.

> I dreamed my son was assembling a new bike (body) in his bedroom (sexual changes in puberty). His dad was very proud of his workmanship. I unintentionally carried the handle bars downstairs. (The mother wasn't giving him steering advice on the use of his new sexual powers.) His older brother carried the handlebars back to him. (His brother is helping him handle this, not necessarily good advice.) Next we were waiting for an earthquake at home.

Waiting for an earthquake indicated there was a shake-up coming. When the mother had this dream she really got suspicious.

> I saw the same son looking lost in a crowd. He had a picture of the girl next door in his pocket next to his heart (she was getting close to him emotionally). On the back of the picture were 'dirty' verses written in a foreign language (couldn't be understood). I heard a voice singing 'Hi-dee, Hi-dee Ho, Hi-dee, Hi-dee Rune.'

While talking to a friend next morning on the phone the neighbor's dog began to bark. The friend asked, "What's that noise?" As the mother said, "That's Heidi, the dog next door," the dream meaning came clear.
The dream was about the 'bitch' next door. She stayed up that night to prove her theory and discovered their rendezvousing. The parents talked with both kids but all were a little shook up. (The earthquake pictured in the first dream.)
Some dreams of the future seem to be psychological

preparation for things we will go through. Others come as warnings to help avert disaster.

> In slumber the eye of the soul waxes bright
> but in daytime man's doom goes unforeseen.
>
> Aeschylus in *Eumenides*

Sheri, a pregnant woman, dreamed that she was having a baby by natural childbirth. She hadn't planned it that way but when the time came her doctor was out of town. By the time another doctor arrived the baby had also arrived, naturally!

Another pregnant woman dreamed:

> I am in the hospital. I have had a miscarriage. My sister is in the bed beside me. She's quite sick and I am telling her it isn't so bad.

She and her sister both had miscarriages. The dreamer's was first and not as difficult. She was able later to comfort her sister.

Some people seem to have a faculty for tuning into emergencies in their sleep, as in these true experiences.

My eight year old son, Brad, was suffering from an extremely severe case of poison oak. The boy and I had spent two sleepless nights. On the third night he finally fell asleep. I left the bedroom doors open and fell asleep in my room. About three hours later Brad woke up. He knew how tired I was and decided to put the medicine on himself. His eyes were swollen nearly shut and the medicine would blind him if it got into his eyes. A very loud dream voice broke in on my sleep of exhaustion, calling my name, "Janice! Janice!" I leaped from bed seeming to know what was needed. One bounce landed me at the bathroom door. Brad had the medicine applicator about an inch from his eye!

Dream help of this kind between mother and child or other relationships where the love tie is strong is not uncommon. This next experience is more unusual because there was no love tie, but there was an emergency.

I had a girl friend who was dating a man, Mr. F. Jr. She had told me a lot about him and his father, Mr. F. Sr., but I'd never met them. One night I dreamed.

> I am in my kitchen cooking because Mr. F. Sr. is coming to dinner. Mr. F. Sr. seemed to be sick and I had an idea I could help him if I could see him and lay my hands on his shoulders. I just felt I could heal him. I wanted to practice bringing the power into my hands before he arrived. I went out into the backyard and sat on our brick wall. Holding my arms shoulder high and straight out in front I said, "Power come!" Then a strange sensation of power like a surge of electric current flowing out through my hands began to flood my being. I felt sure I would be able to heal Mr. F. Sr. when he arrived for dinner.

I awoke with the sensation of the current vivid in my memory. I noted the time as I began writing this strange dream in my journal. It was 2:50 A.M.

The next morning my girl friend phoned and started telling me about the hectic night she had been through. She and Mr. F. Jr. had come to his house where he was living with his father. They got into a terrible argument with Mr. F. Sr. At about three o'clock her boy friend had his arm back ready to swing and strike his elderly father. Then she said "a strange sensation permeated the room." Mr. F. Jr. turned and stumbled onto the couch where he lay in a stuporous slumber.

This is one of those times I'm glad I'm not a scientist so I don't have to try to explain this or pass it off as coincidence. Maybe it has something to do with the phenomenon of healing by 'laying on of hands'. I don't know; I've never done 'laying on of hands'. But something helpful happened and my sensational dream seems to have been a part of it.

In a similar vein I had another dream with that same tingling, electrified sensation which seemed to produce an actual physical healing. I had been having a good deal of trouble and discomfort with my contact lenses, especially in the right eye. It was so bad that I made an appointment for an eye examination. The appointment was for Tuesday. When the trouble started, since I had to wait out the week-end and Monday, I began a program of prayer. On Monday I stayed home from work because of the pain. During an afternoon nap I had this dream.

> I am looking at a bubble of water on our patio. A fish is swimming in it. I feel very awake yet I know this cannot be reality. The bubble changes to a spot of light with a dark center. It begins to move toward me. I am very glad that I am going to be immersed in that light.

> As the light reaches me I feel a tingling, electrified sensation strongly centered in my right eye.

When I awoke the pain was gone. I consider my eyes to be very precious so I went in for the examination anyway. Both eyes checked out fine.

A mother awoke from a frightening dream remembering only that it was about a particular son in great danger. The dream's emotional impact was vivid although the details were forgotten. Down on her knees she prayed for his safety. The next morning she received a telegram. He thanked her for waking him just in time to escape the flames which engulfed the hotel where he was sleeping. He had dreamed he heard her voice and felt her shake him.

A similar thing happened to me although this was a daytime warning. My husband worked in the fire department in Burbank, California. I never knew when he was at a fire or just busy around the station—except one day.

It was late afternoon. I was in the living room with our small children. Something in our bedroom made a loud crashing noise. I hurried in to check on it. There was my husband's large round baby picture, fallen from where it had hung for the past five years. The glass was shattered. A very eerie feeling came over me, somehow I knew he was in danger, maybe even dead! As quickly as I could I rehung his picture on the wall. Then I began to pray most earnestly. Later I received a call from another fireman's wife—they were fighting

the worst hill fire in Burbank's history. I went outside
and saw the smoke covering the hillside.

When Dick got off duty he called and told me what
had been happening. Late in the afternoon of the fire-
fighting, probably at the same time the picture fell, he
and his partner had been caught on a hillside with the
flames advancing rapidly. The wind shifted just in time
and he escaped injury though his partner was badly
burned. Synchronicity and a call to prayer! I wonder
how many times such things go unnoticed?

Another personal experience which was a real life
saver involved all of my children. After a fellow teacher
had surgery she asked me to meet her part way to
school and pick her up. She felt that thirty miles one
way was too far for her to drive for awhile. Because I
worked so far from home I had enrolled my children
there so they were always with us. We chose to leave her
car in a small parking lot in front of three small stores.
This routine continued for about two weeks. One
morning she called and said, "Let's not meet there anymore. I think the store owners may be getting upset.
Let's leave my car around the next corner on the resi-
dential street." "Okay with me," I said.

So that morning I drove on past our usual meeting
place. While picking up Mabel a block away we heard
an enormous crash. At precisely that time a small
plane having engine trouble crashed into the lot where
we had been meeting!

I asked Mabel how she knew. "It was a dream," she
said, "but I didn't want to say so because I wasn't sure
it would really happen."

"Thank God you acted on it anyway," I said. That is a lesson in guidance my children have never forgotten. Every once in a while events like this get into the newspaper. Most people think they could never happen to them, but don't be too sure. Here are more examples that it pays to listen for physical guidance in dreams. You too have a nightwatchman on duty.

This example is reprinted by special permission from the *National Enquirer*. Lee Merriwether, the actress who portrays the secretary on the TV show "Barnaby Jones," had a warning dream before a guest appearance on the "Mission: Impossible" show. She feels this dream probably saved the life of Peter Lupus, star of "Mission: Impossible."

> I dreamed that I was on top of a building, looking down. But instead of being small, the people down below appeared normal size. Then Peter came up the fire escape to rescue me. When he reached me, the fire escape started pulling away from the building. I screamed and reached out for Peter, but he fell.

About a week after the dream, during the guest appearance Miss Merriwether was called on to film a scene on top of a mock-up building which had been constructed on the "Mission: Impossible" sound stage.

"I walked up the steps to the rooftop," she said. "And when I got to the top and looked down, it was just like my dream—the people looked big instead of small. I started to cry and begged everyone to stay off the fire escape.

"Greg Morris ran over and helped me down from the roof, and I went to my dressing room.

"Meanwhile, the stage crew checked the fire escape and found it really was loose.

"If Peter had climbed it like he was supposed to, it would have fallen and injured him seriously. But thanks to my ESP (dream), no one got hurt."

The Fire*

Mr. Williams, an eminently pious man, who lived at Kiddermister in the last century, records in his diary a remarkable interposition of providence of God, in preserving his family and property from devouring flames. One of his servants dreamed that a neighbor's house was on fire, and through the agitation which the dream occasioned she made a little noise, which awoke Mrs. Williams, who was sleeping in a room below. On awakening, she found her room filled with smoke; and when Mr. Williams arose and examined the house, he found part of one of the lower rooms on fire; which, but for the singular manner in which they had been disturbed, would have speedily placed the whole family in danger; and, as the house was not that year insured, have deprived the good man of nearly all he possessed.

— Mr. William's Servant 18th Century.

*From *Gates of Horn and Ivory: An Anthology of Dreams,* compiled by Brian Hill (Taplinger Publishing Company 1968). Copyright © 1967 by Brian Hill. Reprinted by permission.

Mr. W. dreamed.

> I am having a snack in my office, jam
> and crackers and coffee. My older sister
> appears and says, "Don't eat those crackers
> and jam. Danger in it."

A few weeks later his secretary brought him a snack of
crackers, jam and coffee. He remembered the dream
and how that older sister always had to care for him
when he was growing up. So he checked through the
jam and found a piece of jagged glass!

His nightwatchman had been on duty! Listen for
yours.

Chapter Three

Dollars and Sense

The famous psychic, Edgar Cayce, said that financial guidance from dreams is possible. One of the persons he helped through dream interpretation became a millionaire as a stock broker. An example of the type of dreams and interpretations in this series is this Cayce reading numbered 137-24.

> Question-2 [Dream]: . . . "Saw Buchanan, who is a specialist in corn products, on the floor of the New York Stock Exchange. He went to Horace Block, in Block, Maloney's office, and said, 'I have sold four thousand shares of Corn Products and it is now down four points,' and Horace Block answered, 'I am short on Corn Products.'"

Cayce's interpretation:

> Answer-2: "In this we see correlated with that condition as has been given in regards Corn Products. The specialist selling off shows the condition as will first exist, before the commodity would become a buy. Selling then at the 32-33. These, then, would become a buy . . . then we will find

> the advance to the 4 or 6, or 8 points, see?
> Then take advantage of same, not beyond
> that of these changes. Be satisfied with the
> 4 to 6 points . . ."

Notice the name of the office in the dream which told him to get a *block* of corn product stock! Can ordinary people without a psychic's help use their dreams for financial help? Yes, our examples will show that it has been done.

John had worked for North American Aviation for several years. Through profit sharing he had acquired about thirty shares of stock, mostly bought at fifteen to twenty dollars per share. Soon after North American and Rockwell Corporation merged to become North American Rockwell he was laid off. This was a bad time for the aerospace industry but John kept hoping he'd get some profit from that stock. Finally the stock had hiked up to thirty-five dollars per share. John thought perhaps now was the time to sell. He had this on his mind when this dream arrived. For this dream you need to know that sometimes in dreams the right side indicates action and the left side indicates passiveness. This seemed to be one of those cases.

> I am watching a group of people hiking
> in a swamp. (Swamp is a place of unsure
> footing and John was not much of a stock
> market person so he felt unsure of the
> situation.) As I watch I see an old man
> version of myself. I know he is feeling in-
> sulted by something a child has said. (John's
> hurt feelings when the newborn North
> American Rockwell Corp. laid him off.)

The old man feels so bad he holds his nose and walks off to the left into the swamp and drowns himself. The normal me after seeing this happen walks off to join a group of hikers going to the right. Others in the old man's group continue going to the left.

The group I am with, the ones on the right, come back to a lodge on the edge of the swamp. We are waiting for the group from the left to return. They are overdue and everyone is worried. Then I tell them how I saw the old man drown himself. Some of our group go out to search for the lost hikers who went to the left. I stay with the ones in the lodge who have prepared food. The others weren't found. We sat down and ate.

John took this dream to mean: Go with the action to the right, and it will mean food on the table. Stay in the swamp and you'll drown. This may sound far-fetched but it worked for John. He sold the stock at thirty-five dollars per share and North American Rockwell stock never got that high again.

Here is another stock market dream from the Edgar Cayce files since I don't personally know any real stock investors who are watching their dreams. But if they aren't they should.

Question-1. Thursday, October 1, 1925, at home: "I was using my camera to take 'Title' pictures for my moving picture machine. Now in taking pictures of 'Titles' you are supposed to move the camera a little to the left. By some error, I moved the camera to the wrong side—to the right, and only got half of the 'Title' I was trying to take in the picture."

Answer-1: This, as we see, is the correlating of the physical conditions as pertain to those developments of the entity in relation to the commodities that relate to moving picture securities, and only half the quantity of the necessary funds to carry same has come to the individual. Necessary, then, that the entity see that the full contract pertaining to same is carried out, see? Do that. A warning, then, of the necessity of looking into the full workings of that concern in which the body finds self interested, see? Know the whole side, both in and out. Do that."

Edgar Cayce Reading 137-21

This is my story, I call it 'The Case of the Unreal Real Estate.'

Dick and I were spending a quiet evening at home. Then the phone rang!

Dick—"That was 'Mr. Deal' on the phone. He's coming over."

Me—"Why, you haven't heard from him in a couple of years. What does he want?"

Dick—"He's putting together a business deal and thinks I'd be interested."

Me—"Well, how about that. Isn't he being a bit nervy after that other deal he got you into?"

Dick—"Oh, that wasn't his fault, it was the gamble we took."

Me—"I'll fix some hors d'oeuvres," I said softly. But

I was thinking, 'Damn! I don't trust that 'Mr. Deal': He must be desperate for a sucker to call Dick again. But he knows Dick's weakness—too willing to gamble, and so friendly and honest himself he never questions the motives of others.'

Dick and 'Mr. Deal' sat and talked late into the night. Meanwhile I went upstairs to bed. I dreamed.

> I am watching Dick and 'Mr. Deal' playing cards with some other men. The card game is a new one, a combination of poker (gamble) and hearts (motives). In the hearts part of the game 'Mr. Deal' passed sneaky cards to Dick. His motive was that Dick would discard these cards he'd passed and this would complete an opening in his hand to match the cards he'd kept. ('Mr. Deal' planned that Dick would play right into his hand.) Dick fell for this trick twice.

I woke up. While recording this dream in my journal I could see it meant 'Mr. Deal' was playing a sneaky hand. He was trying to get Dick 'set-up' to play into his hands. I planned to tell Dick the dream in the morning. But! When I fell asleep I dreamed again.

> I am talking to our neighbor, 'Mr. Broker'. He is a successful speculator in real estate acreage. I tell him about 'Mr. Deal's' land deal in Riverside County. (I found out later that it was a land deal in Riverside County that they were talking about while I was upstairs dreaming.) 'Mr. Broker's' advice was, "Think! Which will develop first, Lancaster or Riverside? Go from there." I knew the answer was Lancaster.

The dream continued. I didn't want Dick to get caught in another 'Mr. Deal' expensive flop, so I dreamed I told Dick about those two dreams. Dick got so mad I was afraid he would kill me.

Our son, a Libra (characteristically reluctant to break the peace, a symbol of diplomacy), was with me. Then I became a plastic bag of sugar lumps. Dick put the bag of sugar, 'Me', out in the rain. My son and I watched the bag sadly but we realized the plastic covering would save 'Me', the sugar.

While recording the second dream I definitely decided not to tell Dick the dreams. It would create too much anger. I would grit my teeth; put on a plastic (false and flexible) covering and be as sweet as sugar.

A few days later:

Dick—"I don't understand Janice, I know you, this thing with 'Mr. Deal' must be driving you nuts. I know you can't stand him and don't trust him. But I want to go into this land deal. I'll need your signature to get some money, I won't do it without your consent, what do you say?"

Me—"I know you don't like me to mention my dream guidance, but, since you're asking me what I think! While you and 'Mr. Deal' were downstairs talking last week this is what I dreamed. I dreamed about 'Mr. Broker', you know how much he knows about land speculation! I dreamed I asked him about land deals in Riverside. He said, 'Think! Which will develop first, Lancaster or Riverside? Go from there.' Well, it's obvious the answer would be Lancaster. I dreamed that before you ever told me this whole thing was about land in Riverside! (dream telepathy) But, I love you and even though I've butted in before, I made up my mind now to let you make the decisions. I'll do whatever you say."

Dick kissed me on the nose and went into the den to watch television. He never brought me the papers to sign for a loan to make the investment. I knew he'd decided against it. Time proved that deal to be another money loser for 'Mr. Deal'.

Some people would say, "Don't be ridiculous. No one would decide the merits of a real estate deal on advice from a dream!" I knew that Dick felt that way too. But the portion of the dreams I told him was based on logic that could not fail to appeal to Dick's reason. Whereas, 'Mr. Deal' was appealing to his gambling weakness. I feel I was well rewarded for my patient devotion to dream study.

Millie, a California widow, became interested in making an investment in Australian land. The sales pitch was tremendous, comparing western Australia of the '70's to California of the '30's. "Yes," said the salesman, "this acreage is among miles of wheat farms at the present, but, in ten or twenty years who knows? Remember the San Fernando Valley! As in America of the past the Australians are saying 'Go west, young man, Go west!' "

To save the salesman another trip Millie agreed to give him a postdated down payment check. She told him she wasn't quite sure and wanted to sleep on it.

Being widowed and not experienced in real estate investment she really felt in need of guidance. Her ears told her it was good, and she'd seen fortunes made in California real estate. Still, she didn't really understand the group money leverage system the salesman described. Millie felt this problem justified putting a blunt question to her subconscious mind. That night Millie used dream incubation for solving her problem. It worked! She had two answering dreams that night.

> (1)   I saw a vast stretch of wheat fields. A tree grew up in the middle of the wheat. A hand appeared and reached out to pick peanuts from this tree.

The meaning was easy to see. The growth, symbolized by the tree, would be mere peanuts, a slang expression for a very small profit.

> (2)   A friend named Mr. Myers gave some money to an eight year old boy I know named J. West. He sent the boy to take the money to his office. On the way some thugs appeared and the boy dropped most of the money and ran.

The main characteristic of this Mr. Myers was carelessness. The dream seemed to say, 'My ears (sounds the same as Myers) led me to do something careless with my money. 'Go west' was an expression the salesman used, but in the dream the boy named West lost most of the money!

Millie decided against the investment and stopped payment on the check. A couple of months later she met a real estate broker at a party. Millie asked him about the type of group investment leverage system this deal had involved. He told her that really meant the company officials would get most of the profit. Now Millie understood about the thugs in her dream.

From history we find this dream recorded having to do with selecting the site for St. John's College, Oxford, England.

The College*

Sir Thomas White, Alderman of London, was a very rich man, charitable and public spirited. He dreamt that he had founded a college at a place where three elms grow out of one root. He went to Oxford, probably with that intention, and discovered some such tree near Gloucester Hall, he began to repair it, with a design to endow it. But walking afterward by the convent where the Bernardines formerly lived, he plainly saw an elm with three large bodies rising out of the same root: he forthwith purchased the ground, and endowed the college there, as it is at this day, except the additions which Archbishop Laud made, near the outside of which building in the garden belonging to the president, the tree is still to be seen.

Sir Thomas White 1492–1567
Lord Mayor of London

*From *Gates of Horn and Ivory: An Anthology of Dreams,* compiled by Brian Hill (Taplinger Publishing Company 1968). Copyright © 1967 by Brian Hill. Reprinted by permission.

Bruce, a young single fellow, was debating whether to buy a condominium or continue paying out rent on his apartment. He looked at several. Then he dreamed:

> A hand appeared with a card that had on it the address of one of the condominiums he liked. The hand gave the card to his girl friend.

He purchased the concominium. Later while living at that address he married that girl. When they had a baby they sold the condominium. Bruce was very glad he hadn't paid out any more money in rent. This way he had a nice down payment on a home for his family.

Later a friend of Bruce had need of similar advice and it came through in Bruce's dreams. Mike had recently been divorced and was living in an apartment. He hadn't thought of using the cash from the split of their community property. Bruce dreamed up this use for his idle 'dough', money that is.

> Mike was sitting on a couch in the condominium I used to own. On the opposite wall, facing Mike, was a group of pictures made from bread-dough. There were two large figures molded from this bread-dough and framed, also, there were three small figures. I came into the room and saw Mike admiring these pictures. I said, "Do you like those figures? I have the recipe for the bread-dough if you want it."

Bread and dough are two slang expressions for money. Bruce felt the dream suggested a recipe for Mike's money. The dream was set in his condominium and he'd been happy about owning it rather than paying out a lot of rent. He felt it was a good set-up for a single fellow. So he suggested to Mike that he think about getting a condominium. Mike found one he liked in the same development where Bruce used to live. It cost a five figure amount. Though Mike is not a dream enthusiast he thanked Bruce for the suggestion saying, "Good advice is good advice, no matter where you get it."

The *National Enquirer,* on July 7, 1974, reported an interesting case of dream guidance. The dream came to Mrs. Caddy of Findhorn, Scotland. She and her husband founded Findhorn in 1962. It is on a finger of land surrounded on three sides by the sea. Often the cold sand dunes are swept by sixty-mile-per-hour winds. The latitude is about fifty-eight degrees north. In spite of these extremely harsh weather conditions and the sandy soil, she dreamed that they should plant a garden in a certain spot near their home. The growth is incredible including forty pound cabbages. Now many families in the village they founded market produce from their gardens. An expert on soil was quoted as saying, "No known methods of organic cultivation would work in this bleak and barren area." But because of a dream they tried and succeeded in producing for market.

This next business dream is also reprinted by permission of the *National Enquirer;* it is a great example of the financial possibilities of dreaming.

Mrs. Pansy Essman literally dreamed up a thriving business for herself.

She had a startlingly accurate dream one night of a new bath aid for babies and it turned her from a $3-an-hour assembly line worker into the owner and president of a manufacturing company producing 20,000 bath aids a month.

"It all began Nov. 15, 1963," said the 56-year-old grandmother. "I was helping my daughter Caroline bathe her newborn daughter Letha. The baby was terrified of the water and it took the two of us to hold her in order to wash her. We got soaked.

"That night I thought about how hard it was to bathe Letha. After I went to sleep

> I dreamed about bathing a baby. I dreamed I went to my closet and pulled out a pillow-like piece of sponge that conformed to the baby's body. I placed the baby in it and bathed her. She laughed and splashed and her bath was a pleasure.

"The dream was so vivid that I woke up and realized that I had found the answer to the problem that many mothers face with newborns."

Mrs. Essman decided to go into business for herself making the baby bath aids. After six months of looking she had the right sponge-like material that is washable, non-allergenic and colorful. And so the Pansy-ette Infant Bath Aid was patented and the company Pansy Ellen Products, Inc. was born.

Mrs. H., a widow, was a life tenant under the terms of her husband's will. Unfortunately there were some liens against the property. Her lawyer was at a loss how to arrange for her to live her last years in security. One night he dreamed about using a certain legal maneuver to transfer the money burdens from the property onto the capital funds of the estate. It hadn't been done before that he knew of, but it seemed he had dreamed up the solution to his client's financial problem. The judge approved the switch. One more case of financial dream guidance.

A question that may occur to some readers about this time is — why not dream the horse race winners and make a lot of money? In my experience I haven't had any friends or students interested in that endeavor. In Mary Montieth's *A Book of True Dreams* published in 1929 she cites eight cases of people who dreamed about winning horses prior to the races involved.

One of the most interesting was about a young woman racing enthusiast. *She dreamed* that she was discussing the Liverpool Cup Race with a friend. She was wondering how she could pick a winner. The friend suggested that she use the method of opening the Bible at random and pointing to a spot on the page to get a clue. So *in the dream* she did this. She read this passage, "They shall shoot out their lips and their tongues shall be as poisoned arrows."

Sure enough there was a horse entered in the Liverpool Cup named Poisoned Arrow. She told several of her friends about the dream. When they checked, the odds were so great that all were afraid to make a bet on him. Poisoned Arrow won the race!

Concerning horse races I had an interesting personal

experience with a ouija board. In my opinion dreams are a more natural and safer way to tap the unconcious abilities of the mind so I gave up using a ouija board. It seems a tricky business. This is what happened to us.

My friend, Joyce, and I were having a session with Ouija. My husband, Dick, came in and started to tease us. But Ouija had been spelling things for us so we said, "Don't knock it 'til you try it. Ask a question." He did.

Dick—"Will I get the money to buy an airplane?"

Ouija—"Horse race"

Dick—"When?"

Ouija—"Week end 5 Tuesday" Coming after the week-end was Tuesday March 5th.

Dick—"March 5th?"

Ouija—"Yes

Dick—"Bet this Tuesday?"

Ouija—"Yes"

Dick—"Bet on who?"

Ouija—"Aqua Vit Tuesday 8th 5, 8"

Dick—"Is Aqua Vit running March 5th?"

Ouija—"Somewhere, Ha ha."

Dick—"Where is somewhere? What track?"

Ouija—"urs". Ouija always gave us u for you.

Dick—"How much should I bet?"

Ouija—"10 u name it lunch money or super sum ha ha trap a winner"

Dick—"I have to work Tuesday. Should I go to the race?"

Ouija—"Oh no"

Dick—"Should I send the money?"

Ouija—"hot one call Tuesday to the trup t6" A T-6 is one kind of plane Dick wanted to buy. We never did figure out what trup meant.

Dick—"What is T-6?"

Ouija—"for u Easter gift form u to u." Ouija misspelled from.

Neither Joyce, Dick nor I ever paid any attention to the horse races. But we were intrigued. After checking out the racing forms we found that a horse named Aqua Vita was running in the eighth race on March fifth at the nearest track! Amazing! Dick called a friend who was a racing enthusiast and set it up to have twenty dollars bet on this horse and race. What happened? Aqua Vita was scratched! As I say, a tricky business. Still a lot of consciously unknown, factual, future information did come to us from somewhere! None of us knew that such a horse existed much less when and where he was scheduled to race.

Back to our principal subject, financial dream guidance. Another form this takes is in the finding of lost articles. I've read several dreams concerning missing wills or documents needed to settle wills. A friend dreamed her lost ring was between the seat and arm of a stuffed chair, but, she didn't recognize the chair. A few days later she was in the lobby of a restaurant where she occasionally breakfasted. Suddenly she recognized the chair of her dream. The ring was there!

Linda was ironing when her neighbor came by for coffee. Linda excitedly showed her friend the heirloom necklace which her grandmother-in-law had given her on a recent trip back east. Linda's brother and three sailor friends dropped by while the women were talking. Then it was time to pack up her six year old daughter and send her off for a week-end of camping with her cousins.

When everything settled down Linda remembered the necklace. Just as she feared, she hadn't put it away in her drawer! She searched everywhere. The unknown sailors with her brother really had her worried — maybe one of them had stolen it. That would have been easy in the confusion. She was afraid to tell her husband. That night she dreamed.

> I am ironing. When I take some finished blouses to the closet I see something on an empty hanger. It is the necklace!

She jumped up and went to the closet to check. Yes, it was there, looped over a hanger. She found out later that her daughter had put it there and hung it in the closet.

In ancient as in modern days some men trusted dreams to help guide their fortune and others didn't. Or so one form of ancient folktale indicates. These tales tell about a man who is in financial trouble. Then he dreams of a distant place to go and dig up a buried treasure. When he arrives at the spot shown in the dream he finds no treasure. While lamenting his fate a native of the city he is visiting appears and speaks to him. Upon hearing that he came a great distance to find treasure just because of a dream, the stranger begins to laugh. "How foolish!" he says. "I've dreamed three times a similar dream but I haven't gone chasing

after a mere dream. I dreamed about a place in—
(you guessed it, the first dreamer's hometown) where
there is a treasure at such and such a spot." The first
dreamer knows of the spot, returns to his hometown,
digs up the treasure and lives happily ever after!

Everyone knows that the political administration
has a lot to do with the financial situation. Dreams
know that too. Here is an example from history to
show that side of dream intelligence. Richard Heath
was an English businessman.

The New King*
But what promise did Edward VII offer? . . .
Richard Heath, who was given a dream, sum-
med up the change in his sleep. He dreamed
that,

> *He was riding on the top of a horse
> bus with his partner in his engrav-
> ing business. Suddenly a portly gog-
> gle-eyed figure approached them
> and tapped him on the shoulder.*
>
> *'I beg your pardon,' said the
> Prince of Wales. 'But I've come out
> without any money. Can you lend
> me half a crown?'*
>
> *Richard Heath immediately pro-
> duced the coin. The Prince of Wales
> —King Edward—received it with*

*From *Gates of Horn and Ivory: An Anthology of Dreams,* compiled by Brian
Hill (Taplinger Publishing Company 1968). Copyright © by Brian Hill 1967.
Reprinted by permission.

a guttural thanks and hurriedly got off the bus without paying his fare.

Richard Heath's partner, who had remained silent, then spoke up.

'You'll never see that half-crown again,' he said.

— Richard Heath 1832–1912
Engraver and author

Chapter 4

Job Inter-views

Double; double toil and trouble.
Fire burn and cauldron bubble.
                    from *Macbeth*

> Look, Carol, there's the new boss out in
> front of the office. What do you suppose
> he's doing that for? Having batting prac-
> tice with those kids. Doesn't he look ridicu-
> lous in that Mickey Mouse sweatshirt!! And
> look! The Mickey Mouse face keeps chang-
> ing its expression.

This dreamer had thought her new boss was a nice
guy and that he would be great to work for. Time
proved the dream to be correct. Everything he did was
'Mickey Mouse'! He batted things around and kept
changing his form of expression, but it was always of
'Mickey Mouse' caliber!

Creativity and problem solving are a large part of
most jobs, but that aspect will be covered in this book's
chapter on creative mental activity. In this chapter we

will discuss how dreams guide people in choosing work, changing jobs, holding jobs and defining problems at work. This is an area where precognition is prevalent. Consciously we may not tune into happenings and attitudes in others as they are developing but at night, in our sleep, our intuitions are putting it together and bringing it to our attention.

Job insecurity comes to haunt most of us at one time or another. Jill, a competent but apprehensive teacher had this dream the night before the annual visit from the state director of her special teaching program:

> The city supervisor was lecturing and listing on the blackboard the sequence and elements of a perfect lesson plan. She said, "Have your students investigate, reiterate, extrapolate, assimilate and regurgitate."

Jill and I had a good laugh that morning before the state director arrived. As I pointed out to her, "Jill, you do that all the time and it *is* a perfect lesson plan! Your dream is saying, 'Relax, you know perfectly well what to do.'"

The following dream was printed in *Fate* Magazine as a True Mystic Experience feature because of its precognitive nature. It is reprinted here by special permission of *Fate* Magazine.

It is my own dream! In order to be accepted by *Fate* Magazine there had to be an affidavit that witnesses were aware of the dream and its interpretation before the events took place. I had told the dream to several friends as soon as I figured it out which was a year before the job change!

In the past two years most of us have had some association with a person who is or has been unemployed. But only those in the immediate families know what psychological devastation unemployement causes for the victims and their families. In 1963, my husband, Richard, an aerospace engineer, was out of work for nine months. So when heavy unemployment hit the space industry two years ago I naturally started to worry.

Then in June 1969 I had an important precognitive dream. (At this time several men in my husband's department at North American Rockwell in Seal Beach, Calif., had been laid off.) In my dream:

> I saw two of Richard's co-workers, Dale Hansen and John Griscom, in a meadow atop a cliff overlooking the ocean. They were strapping a one-man jet pack on his back sending him, it seemed, on a short trip north along the coast.

The moment I awakened I was sure the dream had something to do with my husband's work. I concluded it meant that when only these three men were left in the department, Richard would be transferred to the Los Angeles plant, 30 miles north. Therefore he would not be unemployed.

A few months later, of the 14 men in Richard's department, only the three in my dream were still working there. In February 1970, North American Rockwell won the contract for the B-1 bomber models to be built in Los Angeles and this confirmed my idea that he would be transferred there. Thus I felt I really didn't have to worry about his being out of work.

In June 1970, a year after I had had the dream, we were invited to a party at Tom Crandall's home in Palos Verdes. We made the drive with John Griscom and his wife and on the way we passed a meadow atop a cliff overlooking the ocean. It was the one I had seen in my dream!

At the party Mrs. Griscom asked me how I felt about my husband being put on 'open transfer.' I gulped and said he hadn't told me. When I cornered Richard he confessed. This party was his 'send-off.' July 13 would be his last day at North American Rockwell and there wasn't an opening for him in the Los Angeles plant.

Naturally he had put out the word of his availability to some of his friends who had been laid off early in the slump and had been hired by other companies. Through one of these contacts, he was interviewed and hired by Hughes Aircraft in Los Angeles to start work August 1. My conclusions from the dream were wrong as to the company and the transfer — but I was right in thinking he would be working a short distance north along the coast. As for the jet pack in my dream, Richard is working on the F-14 and F-15 jets.

The dream kept me from worrying throughout the period from June 1969 to August 1970. My unconscious mind somehow knew what was to come and also how much my conscious mind needed the psychological support of that knowledge. — Huntington Beach, Calif.

Sometimes people are in jobs that are not best suited to themselves. Dreams may suggest job changes. A high school English teacher responded to this dream prodding, took a few more graduate courses, and became a much happier community college instructor of psychology. The dream:

> I'm in the park of my childhood hometown with my brother (alternate life pattern). There are lines of people along the side of the park on Grand Avenue (a grand place to be chosen for the dream setting). There are lines for registering to take college classes. My brother gets in the line to become a psychologist. I think this is a great idea and join that line also.

Psychology has proven to be a Grand Avenue for him to follow.

An engineer who was considering relocating in another state had this dream:

> I saw a commercial airliner that couldn't take off because its tires were flat—they needed inflating. (An accurate picture of his commercial situation. He wasn't getting off the ground. His wallet was flat and in need of inflating.) Next a large train came around the curve (change in direction). My family car was on the track in front of the engine. The train engineer was getting credit for driving the car. I felt concern about the condition of the track ahead of the train. It became a road not a track and the snow (wife's coldness toward the move) had been shoveled away. *I could see a smooth road ahead!*

A dream student with concerns about entering certain job training had this dream:

> I'm in some kind of training school. We have to take a physical fitness test. We have to go over an obstacle course built of white concrete. (This is a concrete route. Nothing nebulous here!) At the end of the course we meet in a cafeteria (a place to get nourishment). Mrs. Baylis (dream instructor) is there conducting a meeting. I'm not pregnant but I'm wearing my old checked maternity smock.

Her instructive dreams have checked this, she is fit. It is a nourishing and pregnant idea, full of promise for her personal birth and maturity.

Anne was considering whether or not to enter training for a specialized type of counseling work. She dreamed:

> I am there at one of the training workshops. I read some of my work aloud to the group. The director came over to me and said, "I think you are one of the most mature ones here." Anne told him she had applied for the special training. He was happy about it. The director wanted to take one of Anne's work papers home to read more carefully so they went to her room to get it. She found herself topless and braless but she was not embarrassed. They went into another room where the director helped her bundle up old newspapers to clear them out of the house.

The director's comment that she is mature enough to do this counseling work is literal enough. Anne will be well accepted. That she could read aloud to the group says much about Anne's conquering her introversion. The dream says the exposure to others will not bother her. Being topless and bra-less but not embarrassed meant to Anne she was liberated. As to the old newspapers, she must get rid of the old news. Don't continue the old line of work—go on into this type of work.

Anne did, indeed, pursue this avenue of psychology much to her own benefit and that of her clients.

A typist whose job had become merely mechanical and unfulfilling had this dream reviewing her situation. Her dream:

> I discover my arm is transparent and I can look through the skin at all the veins. It is like a mechanical arm and I wonder how I will be able to go to work and type the next day. I go to my Mother and ask her why she didn't tell me my arm was like this. She said to me—you were doing just fine and didn't seem to be bothered by it so I didn't see the point in telling you. I felt anger and frustration.

She finally left those vain (vein) efforts and went on to a more satisfying and creative job.

Another girl who was not identifying or feeling a sense of attunement with her work had this clever dream.

> At work with fellow workers (shows the area of concern, her job). Next we are at a

> fair (a place to exhibit products of work).
> Everyone's listening to their own transistor
> radio. They won't tell me what is going on
> because they're afraid they might miss
> hearing something. I'm the only one with
> no radio. (She's the only one not tuned in!)
> Everyone has a wallet and identification
> card. I'm the only one with no identifica-
> tion card. I needed to get one. (She doesn't
> identify with this group, but needs an iden-
> tity.) All the wallets unfold in different
> ways.

(In the ways of the money world, everyone has a different way of unfoldment.) She went on to find another job which she feels holds promise of greater unfoldment for her.

However, not all job frustrations are cause to quit. Often dreams urge us to 'hang in there' even though things are really getting 'screwed up.' Witness Sam's dream:

> A small leather strap was being screwed
> into my right side. It was decided not to
> install one on my left side. I looked back in
> awhile and the screw had come out. I took
> the strap off.

He was working on a project and one worker was screwing things up. This constricted, strapped the action and monetary returns. Remember—right side is the action side. If he did not get his feelings (left side) screwed up it would undo itself! Sam hung in there and kept cool emotionally. The situation worked itself out.

June, an ad saleswoman for a small independent

newspaper, was upset with her new supervisor. She knew he was doing wrong and she felt like quitting though ad selling jobs were hard to find. She dreamed:

> I had a small piece of red plastic Oriental grillwork. My new sister-in-law (whom I'd recently accepted happily as my brother's new wife) said, "Don't break it. You can photograph it and use it as part of an ad."
>
> I noticed it was already broken but I patched it and took it to the lay-out artist and he used it for an ad.

The plastic Oriental grillwork which June described as airy and flexible seemed to bare a combined message. She should orient and grill herself to be flexible and accepting of new family members. Even in the office family. Don't break up the situation; picture how to make use of it. She had already been bitching at work but it wasn't too late to patch things up.

She decided to accept the situation and to be flexible and artistic in how she applied herself. In about three months, the management began to see how her new supervisor was putting the department in the red financially. The old supervisor was rehired and June was so glad she had not quit her job.

Sometimes it is only our own thinking that needs to be changed. That was the case with C.S. who was on the verge of quitting a good job in a medical lab. Her dream:

> It was the last hour of work (on the verge of quitting time). My long hair was hanging in my face getting in the way and

making it hard for me to work. (Her long dark negative thoughts had been interfering with her work efficiency.)

I went home and cut my hair short. This is what her dreams suggest that she do (stop those long dark thoughts from coming out of her head and getting in her way!). The dream continued. The next day at work everyone was surprised by my short hair. A nurse (healing influence) came over and said they needed some strands of my hair for a culture they were making. (Her new-style thinking would be in demand—it would be cultured!) I couldn't wait for the experimental culture to grow. I was excited to see if it would produce the healing medication.

By changing her own attitude, she was able to get along better and become more useful, hence more appreciated, consequently happier at her work.

The following dream brought another person's thinking about her job into better focus. "I Did It My Way". . . .

My supervisor, fellow workers and I were at a meeting. The supervisor gave me many brown boxes of instructional cassette tapes and told me how to arrange them in my office for distribution. I tried to tell her, her idea was not practical for my situation. She insisted I do it her way. In the dream I thought to myself, "The only time I see her is at meetings: she never comes to my office to see what I'm actually doing. So . . . . I'll arrange them my way.

After all, I'm the one who has to work with them.

As Susan, the dreamer said, "I awoke feeling I'd been given a lesson in diplomacy. I could be agreeable with my supervisor when necessary, but at the same time do what I felt practical on the job. In theory her ideas may sound good, but I have to do what's workable, so I will. I put this new found wisdom into action, and felt surprisingly less guilty and more at ease about being practical while sometimes going against what the supervisor said.

Two weeks later I came to work one morning and found a large box holding 28 brown boxes of instructional tapes. The exact boxes I'd seen in the dream!! This was the first time I had ever received any tapes from my supervisor. When I organized them I did it MY WAY."

Hale Irwin, 1974 winner of the U.S. Open Golf Championship announced this bit of dream encouragement on television during the interview immediately after his victory. "I didn't tell anyone except my wife, but I dreamed a few weeks ago that I won the U.S. Open." Psychological preparation for future events often occurs in dreams.

A more famous professional golf dream is one reported by Jack Nicolas. He has told of a dream in which he was holding his club with a new and different grip. Upon awaking, he tried this new style and vastly improved his game. That is creative-problem solving in dreams as related to work problems. Lucky Mr. Nicolas, his new approach concerned no one but himself.

Sometimes people have good innovative ideas to improve work procedures but if co-workers are involved there may be problems getting new programs going. Here is a series of dreams which guided one worker through the battle of revolution which finally saw her new, effective, creative approach duly installed and appreciated. Since babies often symbolize new ideas, I call this series 'Yes, Sir, That's My Baby'.

Dream 1: Nancy, our dreamer (an introvert), her sister (an extrovert with the tendencies needed to put the idea over to others) and Nancy's work partner were going upstairs (thinking area, mental functions) to vote.

The ballot had a pressed daisy attached. (Daisy is the name of the department supervisor. She would have to be pressed to accept the new idea.)

First question on the ballot: Should the program in question be based on concrete experience? This was a basic premise behind Nancy's new program. Nancy voted yes.

Second question on the ballot: Four squares to choose from, each having the same flower design (blossoming ideas), but in different colors. Nancy voted for the design done in tans and browns (the idea is down to earth), yellow (symbol for mental activity — Nancy had thought the idea through) and orange (symbol for energy — she will need it to get the new program going).

Third on the ballot was a place for the voters' comments. She wrote, "I don't think a worker who does creative innovations for her job needs to be told this" (interpreted as, "you know from your past experience that your ideas work well").

Nancy left the voting building and started to walk away. She remembered she had driven there (she is the driving force behind this new program). She knew *she was on the right street* to pick up her car.

With this encouragement Nancy decided to go ahead with the new idea. After talking about it with her work partner, she decided to present it to the supervisor. The next dream warned her that her work partner, lazy and not willing to make waves, would not support her.

Dream 2: Nancy had a beautiful baby boy (idea for a new activity). Her son (masculine, active part of herself) was helping care for the baby. Someone took a flash picture of the baby (partner's quick look). This made the baby hot and sweaty (it's a hot idea but Nancy would have to sweat it out).

Next, Nancy is putting a clean undershirt on the baby (making it presentable). One arm stuck in the sleeve (partner, stuck in the old ways, won't help).

As predicted, the partner gave Nancy no backing. Without her help, the task of getting the new program going was not easy. Nancy was bothered (bugged) by this to the point of feeling persecuted. This next dream says help is on the way:

Dream 3: Nancy is at a college lecture being given by a talented male, Negro artist (to Nancy, Negroes symbolize persecuted people, and the artist represents her as a creative person).

The artist is leaving and going to a garret room (high level) where the college's Negro artists live. She follows him out. She can see he is very upset and asks him what is wrong. He tells her it's because a refined lady (the partner) had said, "There are no good Negro artists. If they appear to do all right they are either starving or stealing!" (Now that the program was started in spite of the partner, she was belittling it.) In the dream the artist (Nancy) was upset because he was afraid he might meet this lady, lose his temper and hurt her (Nancy was fighting her temper not to argue with her partner).

They got to his room and there were chartreuse bugs on his floor. (Nancy is being "bugged" and in some ways doesn't understand [floor] her partner.) Nancy tries to kill the bugs, but her shoes (understanding) are too small.

(Dream's prognosis and promise:) A large man came into the room behind Nancy (to back her up). He stomped on the bugs with his big shoes. End of dream.

The big man proved to be the boss in charge between the partners and Daisy, the department supervisor. He supported Nancy with regard to her partner, other co-workers and Daisy. He stomped out all opposition and indifference that was bugging Nancy.

That program grew, became strong and Nancy happily refined the details. It became an accepted part of the job which not only made Nancy happier with her working conditions but it greatly benefited the co-workers in her department.

> Dream 4: Nancy and her partner get on a large ship. Nancy has a strong baby boy. They are taking a bath (cleansing) together. Baby wants her to wash him. She lathers him all over and rinses him (clears up details in the program). He is so strong he stands up in the tub, but holds on tight while she washes him. She got him a clean T-shirt. It had a thin, red stripe (only a little anger showing now) between wide, green stripes (green is the color of growth).
>
> It is New Year's Eve (new beginning) and boat owner, who is her boss, is having a party. There are many commercial decorations on the boat. A fellow worker says, "Original decorations (creative productions) are much nicer than commercial ones." As Nancy watched the commercial decorations became originals. One of the co-workers is admiring one which Nancy has made.

From then on it was clear sailing for Nancy's project. It was her 'baby,' and she watched as the fresh idea took hold and grew. Her co-workers accepted and appreciated the originality of her plan. What a difference from the early days when she had to fight to give the plan a chance and her only friend had been her dreams.

This unassertive worker is being reminded not to let others get credit for work she has done, a problem she has had in the past. Her dream:

> When I got to work, I very much noticed Kris is in the office. (Kris is—sounds like Crisis—there was a crisis in her office.)
>
> There was a memo in my mailbox partly made from stickers. (A sticky situation.)
>
> The memo was a scolding to sign in daily and put my signature (identity) on all my work. The L.D.G. (Learning Disability) teacher was in the same trouble. (This dreamer had a hard time learning this lesson about not letting her work get mixed up with other people, whereby they get credit for her efforts.)
>
> I explain to the boss that I forgot and I apologized. My apologies were accepted— end of dream.

The mistakes and inefficiencies at work which cause us problems are not always our own. Often, we are caught up in other people's messes.

One night, Barbara dreamed this uncomfortable dream. It alerted her to a dangerous, but unavoidable situation. Knowing the potential danger, she handled the delicate situation with great caution. Her dream:

> Someone was with me on my right side (action). We were going to clean out an area. I had to reach up over my head and take a book off a dirty shelf. Bunches of black widow spiders crawled out and the other person stamped out several baby ones

that fell on the floor. Two medium-sized
ones were on my lower arm — I pushed
them off and felt relieved. I feared there
was another one somewhere that might bite
before I found it. I felt the other big one
nearer my shoulder; it was very big. I was
very afraid. I pushed it off and woke up.

The very next morning, Barbara's top boss asked
her to take over a chore ordinarily handled by Pam,
who was between them in authority. Pam was out ill
and the top boss was using this opportunity to clear up
a bit of a mess Pam had made. He wanted to get this
done while she was out of the way. In other words,
Barbara had to reach into a mess created by those over
her head. At least the big boss was right beside her. In
this office there was a hierarchy of devouring females
(black widows). Two were especially close to Pam and
if Barbara wasn't careful they would try to do her in for
going into Pam's area of jurisdiction. Needless to say,
Pam could be very dangerous if Barbara was not aware
of where she made her next move. But, forewarned was
forearmed and Barbara managed to satisfy the top boss
without being bitten by the falling black widows.

One teacher who had an instructional aide who was
due for her performance evaluation had this dream
warning of a rocky situation.

Phyllis, my aide, had taken my Scott
Foresman worksheets and filed them in the
front office filing cabinet. I went to ask her
why she did such a dumb thing — we need
them here accessible to us. When I found

her coming out of the office she was wearing a red, white and blue dress with a very
wide ruffle at the bottom. When she saw
how angry I was she began to cry. I felt she
was acting like a big baby. I told her if she
didn't want to keep my papers in my place
she should go buy her own set. She stormed
away. When I got back to our room I found
a bunch of rocking chairs Phyllis had told
the office they could store there until
school was out. It was very awkward trying
to maneuver around the rocking chairs.

The teacher had put one suggestion for improvement on the aide's evaluation — not too bad. Next
morning our teacher found the aide had taken the
evaluation papers (the teacher's foreman type duty) to
the school principal. She was making a federal case
(red, white and blue) out of her ruffled feelings. And
she was being a cry-baby. It made the rest of their year
together rocky and awkward!

A secretary who was having some trouble with one
of the junior executives saw her choices this way:

I'm in a laundry room with the offend-
ing junior executive. Mr. Wiley is standing
behind him. The laundry machine has
only two buttons. One, the adjustment
button, is flashing. The other is a restart
button.

As she saw it, he was treated like a son by the boss,
but was a wily character. If she could adjust to this, as
the flashing button suggested, she could clean up,

launder the situation. The only other choice was to restart which would mean changing jobs. She did finally restart elsewhere but it was a costly move.

All work and no play makes Jack a dull boy.

> I saw a huge round yellow and red tent. It looked like a revival tent but actually it was supposed to be at Disneyland and was a hot dog stand. It belonged to a friend; I said, "Good, maybe we can get cut-rate tickets to Disneyland."

This dream seemed to have a friendly suggestion for our hard-working dreamer. Cut his rate. "Hot dog! Go to Disneyland." (Symbolic of recreation, relaxation, amusement.) See the warm, bright energetic colors of the Disneyland revival tent.

All work and no play makes Jane a dull girl.

> I'm on a bus (public system; this dreamer worked for a public system). A truck with war-time enemies in it is following us. At 12:15 A.M. it will be time for me to escape from the bus. (12:15 A.M. is just beginning a new day.)
>
> It is now 12:15 A.M. and I climb out of a bus window. I am in the country (peace and quiet away from the hustle and bustle of the city). I have a big bunch of balloons (fun time). I see a co-worker and I'm trying not to be seen by her.

This seems to say—get away from the hustle and bustle, escape in the peace and quiet, have a fun time and avoid work for awhile. This is a good interpretation because this dreamer worked too hard and didn't take enough time to relax.

I don't know where the term workaholic came from. I first saw it in an Ann Landers column. Anyway there are many people in America who are overly addicted to work and that is a good term to describe the next few dreamers—workaholics. Most often this affliction is the result of a parental influence which put a high value on work. Many children are made to feel worthless unless they are productively occupied—if not with a job at least with studies.

> The dreamer, hereafter known as Career-woman, was with a friend who was prominent in the same line of work. They were driving the car of Career-woman's parents (parents' influence is the driving force in this activity). The car is chugging, they are taking it to get it repaired. (This driving force is beginning to break down.) The two career-women stop at a factory. They go inside and steal some huge hunks of bologna which will hardly fit inside her parents' car. (This all work is really a 'big bunch of bologna'). Soon after they leave with the load of bologna they are arrested.

This showed her that her heavy work load was a lot of bologna and that it arrested her movement through life.

Here we see the dream pattern of Friend A represents the suggested solution and Friend B represents the bad habit.

> My friend Susan, sociable relaxer, wanted
> to borrow my car. (Play time wants a place
> in her life.) She wanted to use my car to go
> to a party late at night (some 'night life').
> I said, 'No, I think Jerri (workaholic) might
> want to use it. Buy your own car.' Susan is
> dejected and mad at me.

After those dreams this Career-woman made it a
point to get out more at night after work and be more
sociable. It happens to men too. Mr. Volunteer was
always taking on volunteer jobs besides doing his regu-
lar job. His dream:

> I'm going to my volunteers meeting. My
> mother appears and says, "Let's play mo-
> nopoly." Then I'm in my car but 'Mr.
> Other Volunteer' is driving. It is very
> crowded and I can't get enough air. Also
> I can't reach around to roll down the win-
> dow. I'm almost panicky, fearing I will get
> a stiff-neck and claustrophobia.

This extra work is monopolizing his life. He is not in
the driver's seat controlling his life energies. It is crowd-
ing his life and choking off his air. All work and no play
also makes stiff-necked people.

Sometimes people who were raised to feel worthless
unless working expect spouses to treat them the same
way. A Career-woman was having this problem.

> Husband and I were moving son B's
> amplifier out onto the front lawn. Son B
> was a hard-worker too. She was now be-
> coming aware of her work addiction (mov-
> ing the worker's amplifier out into her

> conscious—the front of her mind). My husband and I get into an argument while moving the amplifier.
>
> He says, "You're upset because of the moving."
>
> I say, "I'm upset because I don't mean as much to you as the amplifier. I don't mean anything to you and never can."
>
> He says, "Yes you can when you get that dress your sister is making for you!"

The sister had a better self-image and did not work outside the home! Career-woman's fear and feeling that she was only important as a hard worker was all in her own consciousness. Her husband would love her more if she were like her sister!

Work isn't always of a paying nature. One woman new to A.R.E. study groups dreamed:

> I am selling round and square Edgar Cayce and A.R.E. stickers to people.

She became very active in A.R.E. work!

Another woman who had just become interested in a metaphysical church had this dream:

> An airplane hit some wires near my house. I hear this loud buzzing of electricity. The casualties were brought to my house. I was administering first-aid. My mother and dog were helping. An ambulance was called to take them away.

As she studied with this church group, she learned to channel healing powers. People who are healing channels say there is a sensation of heat and vibrancy akin to electricity. Her mothering instinct and desire to be-friend humanity (dog as man's best friend) were help-ing her. But she is only an aid station—the real healing comes from a higher power, Christ the Great Physician.

St. Francis was quite an ordinary man when he started out for the Crusades. But he had dream guid-ance which turned him around to battle within the politics of the church. He had gotten as far as Spaleto on his way to the Crusades battleground when he had this dream.

> "Francis," said a voice, "Where are you going like that?" "I am going to fight in Apulia." "Tell me, from whom can you expect most, the master or the servant?" "From the master, of course!" "Then why follow the servant, instead of the master from whom he takes his orders?" "Lord, what do you want me to do?" "Return to your country; that is where, what you ought to do, will be revealed to you and you will understand the meaning of this vision."

On the basis of this dream, Francis turned back. And waited.

In the Spring of 1206 in the Chapel of St. Damian, Francis had this meditation vision:

> Kneeling before the wooden crucifix, lo the Christ, opening his painted lips and calling him by his name said, "Francis, see to the repairing of My house which is fall-ing into ruin."

Francis pondered on the repairing; he thought he knew what he should do. But there were others to convince. Powerful people. It might even go to the Pope. It did! The dream Francis had before his interview with Pope Innocent III:

> Having come across a large tree with vast, spreading branches, Francis stopped to admire it; suddenly a supernatural force had made him grow as tall as the top of the tree and then he had, without effort, bent the tree down with his hand.

In his eyes, this indicated the ease with which Pope Innocent III would be bent, by the grace of God.

It was true. Even the formidable Pope, bent as the dream had foretold he would. Francis left the Pope with the blessings of the Church on his project of founding the Franciscan Order. For his works, Francis was elevated to Sainthood. Even today he is recognized as the epitome of gentleness and love for all of God's creatures. Guided by his Higher Self, through dreams and meditation he became a saint instead of a soldier.

In no way would I put my church work in the same class as that of St. Francis. But only because of a very interesting dream and synchronistic happening did I have the courage to become ordained.

Precognition flits in and out of our dreams. Often, we only recognize it has come and gone long after it has passed. Such is the following dream which came two years before the event it depicted. Though not understood at the time, the dream left such an impact that when the opportunity came, I felt it right for me to take this important career step. Because I had dreamed the experience in such detail, I felt some part of me was looking forward to this day. The dream:

> There were twin brothers named Paul and Peter. I had known Paul but was to be married that afternoon to Peter whom I had never seen. The wedding was to be held in a hotel in the desert. Guests were coming a distance of 29 miles from opposite directions.
>
> I entered the hotel dining room where some of the guests were eating eggs. I saw Peter come in from the other side. He was young, blonde and handsome. Someone led me out of the dining room quickly because Peter was not supposed to see me before the wedding. He didn't see me.
>
> I was taken to the hotel gift shop and told to choose any piece of jewelry I wanted to wear for my wedding. I chose a large gold butterfly. Then I went upstairs to get dressed and wait for the ceremony.

Two weeks later I was shopping with a friend. I spotted a large gold butterfly made for holding long hair. Even though I had short hair I bought the gold butterfly with exclamations of joy. I recognized it from my dream and knew it had some very special meaning for me. My friend was a little amused and enjoyed my dream story, though she didn't understand it any more than I did. We both adopted a "let's wait and see what it means" attitude.

Sometime later I began taking classes from a religious teacher whom I grew to respect greatly. I began to feel a calling to go into religious teaching but would need to become an ordained minister for that. My teacher and a Bishop from an affiliated church felt I was ready and an ordination date was set. The church was The Independent Church of Antioch founded by St. Paul, and the apostle Peter was first Bishop of the original church. In the ceremony which ordained me as a Missionary Minister in the Independent Church of Antioch, I wore the golden butterfly in my hair which had grown long during the two years of pre-ordination studies.

After the fact, it was easy to understand the symbolism of the dream.

Twin brothers—affiliated churches. Paul represents two people—the teacher I knew and studied with. Also the founder, in Bible history, of the Church of Antioch. Peter represents two people—the unknown Bishop who performed the ordination. Also, the first Bishop of the Church of Antioch. Wedding; marriage—symbolizes the close union and the vows to the church—the ordination. Coming from two directions—it actually happened that five ministers were ordained at that time, three came from one county and two from another. The ceremony was held at a central meeting point. Eggs—new birth; something hatching. Peter—young, blonde and handsome—my idea of an ideal groom. He didn't see me—a traditional belief about a lucky wedding if the groom doesn't see the bride on the day of the wedding. Jewelry—precious possessions. Gold—precious metal. Usually symbolizes attainment. Butterfly is adulthood or maturity arrived at through processes of complete metamorphosis.

Chapter 5

Blood, Sweat and Cheers

The curtain rose on a puppet show. The chorus began its lilting love song, "I'm as restless as a willow in a wind storm. I'm as jumpy as a puppet on a string . . ." The dreamer was amazed as he watched the puppet. Whoever was pulling the strings was keeping his feet off the ground. Poor puppet being held 'up in the air' like that!

As the dreamer drifted closer, he saw that he himself was the puppet!

"Would you like a 'Bloody Mary', dear?"

"Yes, I'll have one."

Gag, cough, spit! Horrors! The drink was filled with glass splinters! He looked unbelievingly into the face of his sweetheart as he clutched at the glass in his throat. She smiled sweetly. He woke up in a cold sweat.

'Cherchez la femme' — She'll cut your throat!

Interpersonal relationships — husband/wife, lovers, parent/child, siblings, friends — these are where life is really lived. We all have blind spots in how we respond to or reach out toward others. The young man who dreamed he was a puppet kept 'up in the air' by a girl-friend who would 'cut his throat' still had difficulty seeing the character of their relationship. He didn't *want* to believe it!

Lest I sound one-sided, here is the opposite sort of picture. A young woman with boyfriend problems had this recurring dream.

> A large pair of men's feet would come out of the drawers of my bedroom chest. The feet would come and walk up and down all over me. Sometimes I knew they were my father's feet, sometimes they were the feet of boyfriends.

Drawers in the sense of men's underpants symbolized male sexual powers. Due to her childhood family life, her image of male/female was that men dominate. Her father had 'walked all over' her mother and herself. She didn't feel men could be expected to be any other way. It took some hefty insights to get her over that blind spot.

People in their desire, nay need, to be loved get themselves into all kinds of unbalanced situations. Usually, I hear about it from the female side, women being more open about their emotional problems. Here is an example of a woman, mother of three children, who had been separated from her husband for ten years but they were not divorced. She took a lover. By nature, she wanted a true family life but the way she had organized her life, it was impossible. Even if her lover wanted to marry her he couldn't. Of course, her dreams were trying to help her. Soon after she met the lover she had this dream which showed that he would be unable subconsciously to accept their adulterous relationship without guilt. Her early dream.

> I was in the family home of my lover. It was a large, luxurious bedroom with high ceilings. The walls and floors were of delicate pastel mosaic. At the window were beautiful white drapes looking like a veil. The bed was the only furniture in the room. I was alone, naked in the bed trying to hide myself with a sheet.
>
> A middle-aged, severe looking woman stood in the doorway. I knew it was his mother. She was talking calmly to me. She said that I was wrong, her son and I cannot love each other. She said that I was to go out of her home. I was crying. She turned to him and asked, "Is she the one you looked all over for?" Slowly he walked toward his mother.

The setting of the dream shows the area of concern male/female relations of a sexual nature as related to the influence of his family background. His understanding, the floor, is a mosaic of many pieces, a complicated design. There are barriers, walls, also built of the complicated design. His family put a high ceiling on bedroom relations. She is alone in the bed; that is, he is not really with her in this affair. The bed being the only furniture indicated that theirs was a sexual relationship only.

During the relationship, this recurrent dream appeared.

> I'm in a house facing the sea. I want the
> house to be mine. I see a man but he has
> no face. The voice is that of my lover; he
> says, "I'll be back" but he disappears.

The sea symbolizes her deep subconscious, facing herself at that deep level she wants a total house, a total relationship, not just a bedroom. But he can't face that total commitment with her. He says he'll be back but he disappears! Actions speak louder than words.

After three years, they broke up their relationship (he disappeared). Then she began having this recurring dream in various forms.

> I meet him on the street always by acci-
> dent. I find the door of his new apartment,
> he is always with friends, never another
> woman. He talks to me about the girl he's
> on his way to see. He laughs at me or he
> makes me do housework while he sits and
> watches.

Her subconscious is trying repeatedly to get her to face reality. How many signs of rejection does she need?

They never have a planned meeting; he taunts her about another woman; who can stand to be laughed *at*; he treats her like a household slave! It's hard to believe but after two years she still isn't convinced. How often we carry the torch until it burns our hands!

Mary had this experience in trying to relate to a man. She started dating him when he was married to his first wife. He got divorced but after a time told her he was not willing to marry again. So she broke up their relationship except for occasional dates. But she kept hoping he'd marry her.

Soon he married another woman with two children and they had one of their own. Mary, meanwhile, is still hoping he'll marry her. She had this dream showing her the error of her thinking.

> I'm walking down a side street back in the town where I used to live (where they dated). The buildings there are shabby. I'm wearing a short black coat and a fur hat. I'm carrying a new red suitcase I just bought. I see him, he is wearing the sport coat he used to wear. He has a fresh hair cut. He is putting much luggage in a truck painted red, white and blue. I know he is taking his family on a vacation. As I pass he says, "Oh, Mary," not as an exclamation, more of a statement, not actually speaking to me. I didn't say hello either.

That part of her life in the past was just a side street, shabby at that. She was vulnerable because her protection, coat, was short and her thinking, hat, was fuzzy. His attitude, clothes, were sporty—he made sport of her. His old type thinking is gone, the fresh hair cut. Red, white and blue are the colors of his homeland. He is relaxing, vacation, even though he needs a truck to pull the load of his family (homeland). His words may suggest to her, Oh marry. The red suitcase she has seems to say, take up the energy (red) you have and travel on! Incidentally, she had this dream on April Fool's Day!

If people could only accept that life is a series of

changes and when one cycle is over, push on. Too often we have a little, or a lot, of psychic or emotional energy tied up in a dead relationship. Then we have less energy to expend in the here and now living as we should be doing.

Then when we have a precious relationship in our hands, how often we crush it. A high school girl dreamed it this way.

> I'm holding a fragile, cute, precious kitten and I really love it but I keep crushing it.

In relating to that dream, she recognized the kitten as representative of her boyfriend. He is cute and she really likes him but often says things that 'crush' him. The dream made her aware of how fragile the relationship was and the danger that she might easily destroy something she held precious.

There is a masculine counterpart to this. Bill's summary of his life at the time was this. Christmas Eve, 197_, beginning of a new love—end of an old love. September 197_, end of a love that was once new. I feel like a "pizza to go." Soon after this, he met a new girl who owned a white V.W., he owned a blue V.W. Then came this dream.

> I'm walking home (home is where the heart is). I'm being pursued by a construction machine and I run through some ditches. The blue and white V.W.'s come along, driving in a sort of dance pattern.
> I feel the impression from the cars of the Chinese Yin-Yang symbol.

If he wants a home, a lasting love, he'll have to quit

ditching constructive pursuits. He should see the girl as a balancing half in the yin/yang, male/female, dance of life.

So much for the lovers, what happens after the knots are tied?

> *Marriage is a legal and religious ceremony by which two people of the opposite sex solemnly agree to harass and spy on each other until death do them join.*
>
> *Elbert Hubbard*

This precognitive dream came three years before Eve's separation and reunion which it foreshadowed.

> I had just finished a long, rough ocean voyage with my husband. We had been moving to a new state away from our parents. I'd been working as a receptionist for three years. We were going to be remarried and I was telling my sister about it.

At the time of the dream, Eve had just started working as a receptionist. Three years later she had been through the rough ocean (emotional) travels of: separation from her husband; changing a lot of attitudes inherited from parents; becoming more receptive and reuniting the family into a different state of living.

Here is a series of other dreams from her journal following this marital problem through that three-year period — just samples along that rough ocean voyage.

> You Brute!
> Three women are hiding from Nazi oppression. I see my husband, Adam, standing on a corner. He is a Nazi officer. He

has a stiff neck and a blind left eye (can't see from his feeling side). A nurse is helping him see. He is writing out a ticket for someone.

The three faces of Eve are oppressed by her unfeeling, stiff-necked husband.

You Idiot!
Eve is stirring a pot of stew. Voice says, "It usually ends up altogether different than what you set out to do."

By 'stirring things up' and 'stewing,' Eve makes a mess!

I Quit!
Eve's family, brothers, sister, parents and children are all together in a high beamed house, lots of windows, light and airy, built by her father (he represents what she expected from marriage). Eve had just poured a cup of hot coffee. Father says, "We are going to have an earthquake." (Shake up the whole family.)
The quake rolled Eve across the floor. When it was over, her father said, "How quickly you put down the hot coffee and got on the floor."

When Eve got a handful of hot emotions (coffee), she left Adam and moved into her own apartment. It shook up the whole family. The dream pointed out, though, that when Eve got rid of those hot emotions and got shook up herself she would get down to some basic understanding (floor is under our feet on which we stand).

He'll Try!

A doctor and his wife (healing influences) arrived late for a dinner engagement at their house. Adam fed them (cooperated) though Eve was mad because they were so late.

She'll Try, Too!

Eve in her new apartment was setting up things to do the ironing (smooth things out). Was debating whether to do it in the living room or in the dining room where it was lighter. Decided on the room with the most light.

By putting light on the problem, things could be ironed out.

Make Peace and Bear Fruit!

Mrs. M, a friend, was giving a lecture on dreams (lesson from the subconscious levels). Adam and Eve went through the lecture hall and then outside to look at their olive tree (peace symbol). It had almost died but was being revived. The infested branches had been wrapped and sprayed (problem was being treated). There were branches bearing ripe olives even now (fruits of their growth).

A woman said, "Your tree also needs nourishment. The teacher, Mrs. M., giving the lecture has the proper formula. When she finishes I'll have her tell you what the formula is." Eve was waiting.

Mrs. M, the friend, was forced by her doctor to quit

work. This was Eve's only association to her as a symbol. Later, Eve quit her job and found it helped the marriage. By using Mrs. M as the instructor in the dream, Eve was being told to emulate Mrs. M and quit work.

Together Again

Adam and Eve are living in a family community being constructed on a hilltop. At a table in the restaurant there a man commented on how well the community project was turning out. He also remarked that Eve was a good leader. Eve replied, "No one is a leader here. Everyone is equal."

Adam led Eve out to a view spot on the hilltop. Jacaranda trees were in blossom. The breeze was pleasant. Eve looked at Adam and sighed, "It isn't as cold as you would expect."

They have constructed a new family relationship on a higher level based on equality. It is pleasant.

And They Lived Happily Ever After . . .

Adam and Eve are driving along together. The sky off to their right was very, very blue and very, very beautiful. The hills and mountains were very green — very clear atmosphere. They could almost see each individual clover. Together they went off the road to find the family picnic, knowing it would be a good day. Someone showed the others at the picnic a doll trophy Eve had won as a 'good for you' type trophy at a previous family picnic.

Life together, with a clear atmosphere, is a picnic, and Eve, you are a 'doll', and 'a winner'!

Eve's dream commentary kept her posted throughout her rough ocean voyage to a mature relationship.

This situation finally ended in divorce, but better the husband should be alerted than continually 'sandbagged'.

> Husband dreamed his wife was out walking along the street about 2:00 A.M. A policeman stopped her and said, "What do you have in your handbag?"
>
> Wife said, "It is sand," and showed him her bag full of sand.
>
> Policeman said, "You're under arrest."

The wife was 'sandbagging' her husband with stories of going out late at night to the laundromat. Two is the number of separation or division—which her activity led to. It should be arrested—stopped.

Often dreams react to the daily events between people, giving intuitive information about their feelings. Watch for what you dream after an argument with your spouse. For example:

> Wife woke singing, "Home, home on the range . . . Where never is heard a discouraging word!"

This was most meaningful to her in light of the previous night's argument about finances and other domestic hassles.

Another similar example:

> Wife dreamed of a friend who had just had a new *baby girl*. The friend, a teacher, was talking to her school principal about the baby. He thought it was wonderful.

> Dreamer's husband came in and talked to her about *them* having a baby girl. He really wanted them to have one *very* much. So the wife said to the friend's principal, "My husband has had a vasectomy so we can't have a baby girl because of him, but he really wants one now very much."
>
> The principal replied, "That's a problem, but I'll see what I can do about it."

The baby girl represents a new birth of feminine characteristics—feelings and emotions. The husband caused the rift to begin with as indicated by dream vasectomy. But now the husband really wants the couple to have a new birth of feeling between them. The wife's principles will try to help her overcome the problems.

Another wife has a less cooperative husband but growth is not impossible.

> Wife dreamed her house was across the street from her husband's house. There were some trees at the side of his house but there was no hose or water at his house. She was planning to come across each day with water from her house. If she did the trees would grow, otherwise the trees would die. She didn't want the trees to die so she began carrying water over in buckets.

She came across in the marriage with the necessary emotional output and fortitude. So, growth did take place on the husband's side—eventually.

> John Doe dreamed he'd argued with his wife (in fact he had). He went to a gypsy

> for a potion to mend the rift. The gypsy
> sold him a jeweled brooch with his wife's
> picture in the center. He was to give this
> brooch to her to wear next to her skin.

The advice was, picture her as a precious jewel and present this picture to her. If she knows you feel she is precious you will be able to get close to her. Gypsies often symbolize instinctual wisdom.

Another husband dreamed he should work on his marriage relationship in a more mature way.

> Husband and wife are *smooching* in bed.
> He turned and saw himself in the mirror.
> His *hair* had almost all turned *white* and
> *gray*. It was cut short and was straight. It
> had just been washed. *He got up to go to
> work.*

His hair was really black and curly. The dream says his thinking (hair) should be colored with maturity, should be straight and should be cleansed. He went to work on his attitude toward the relationship right after that dream.

Most of us need to be told at some time to take better care of our precious relationships. A domineering type woman dreamed it this way.

> I'm shopping at a jewelry store for a chain.
> I have several real precious jewels to put on
> the chain. The shopkeeper turned out to
> be Mrs. X. She showed me a small, thin
> chain. I said, "How can I put my precious
> jewels on such a thin chain? They might
> fall off and get lost! No, I need a stronger
> chain."

Since she was doing the shopping, the dream showed that the needed action was up to her. She had a very precious family but the relationships were getting more and more distant. Mrs. X was a woman with almost no family ties; her husband and children, frankly, couldn't stand her. The chain of events in the dreamer's life, the links to her precious family members, needed to be strengthened or she was in danger of losing them as Mrs. X had. After this dream she became more appreciative of the jewel-of-a-husband she had.

And now the womens' lib movement appears on the shifting sands of time. We need a female king to symbolize this reigning equality of importance for both sexes. For one married and dominated woman that symbol was Billy Jean King. I call this dream "Tennis Anyone?"

> I saw Billy Jean King and knew she had played and won two sets of tennis (recent battles between the sexes in dreamer's married life — she was making progress). I knew a third match was about to be played. Out in the front row of stands were four men in Royal Air Force uniforms (her husband of English descent considered himself quite royal and always put himself out in front). Their wives sat behind them in drab housedresses, unprotected by coats. They were covered in a thin layer of ice. I knew without saying (it goes without saying as a natural order of things) that the husbands had told them it would be warm and *they always did as they were told* and that was why they dressed that way.
> I asked the women to come into my

house for hot coffee. They said, "Yes." I knew they really wanted to see what an American (freedom from English rule) home would be like. Once inside my house, Billy Jean King came to get me and said it was time for us to play tennis (get going and play the womens' lib game). I hurried out to play the game. End of dream — beginning of her liberation.

In ancient times, January 21st, St. Agnes' Eve, was believed to be a night for girls to dream of their future husbands. The girl was to skip dinner that night and see what her dreams foretold. Even though I'm married, I naturally had to try it. Skipping dinner was no small sacrifice but I had this rewarding dream.

My husband and I were now living in a new house on a high level of a hill.

In these days of rampant divorce, it was a comfort and three years later our marriage has reached greater heights.

Behind every marriage is that age old in-law problem; sometimes they act like outlaws. But, Maggie found out how to handle hers.

I was walking through a defense plant and found a large negative on the floor. I picked it up and held it to the light and saw it was a picture of my father-in-law. It was too big to put in the wastebasket so I pinned it on a bulletin board.

Her father-in-law is pictured as negative and defensive. Her dream is putting light on this subject for her.

He is too big a thing in her life to throw out or ignore. What he needs is to be paid attention to; take notice of him. She did and became almost a friend.

A few days after I had this dream my mother-in-law suffered a severe heart attack and I was needed to be close to her as I had been when our children were babies. The dream says: Let my best principles and neighborliness live in this relationship. Bring all my faculties to this problem.

> I'm at my mother-in-law's house. I have the boys with me, but they are babies again. (When they were babies, my mother-in-law cared for them while I worked.)
>
> I'm a teacher and the best principal I ever worked for lives in my mother-in-law's house. He also owned the houses on both sides (is very neighborly). In the dream I remembered his daughter is no longer living at home and my mother-in-law's daughter also is thousands of miles away.
>
> The whole faculty was going into my in-laws' house for a lunch.

Another very vital relationship in life is that between parent and child. The parent should nurture the child as a nurse cares for her patients, but it doesn't always work out to be a healthy relationship. One high school girl dreamed about her sick mother/daughter situation this way.

> I'm in a hospital about to be released (at her age she is about to graduate and leave home). I have to wait for my suitcases (what load of parental influences will she

take with her). I'm looking out the window at some children learning to play baseball (her own childhood and the basis [bases] she learned). The nurse in charge (disguise for her mother) has a generation gap problem with the children. I feel this strongly in the dream.

One little boy (disguise for her childhood self) didn't play exactly right (some of her childish actions were mistakes). The nurse becomes violently angry and shakes the little boy. He is choking on some gum he was chewing.

I start to yell at the nurse. She comes inside and gives me a very painful shot. Then she puts me in an upper bunk (her mother gave her a lot of intellectual bunk). I ask the nurse to bring me a cup of water. (She needs and asks for emotional comfort.) The nurse goes back and forth several times but the cup is always empty when she gets back to me.

Maybe seeing the truth like that will make her a better mother when her time comes. That was an emotionally empty relationship and she felt the pain of it. Too bad her mother wasn't studying dreams.

In another mother/daughter situation, the mother was tuned in to her dreams. This helpful message came to her after a particularly bitter argument with her daughter.

I'm at a convention with a large group of women (she's been doing the conventional things women do). Every woman has a different reason for being there. A very stylish woman asks me my reason, then turns rudely away without waiting for an answer (with mothers it is stylish and conventional to ask but not listen!).

I tell her I am a shoe saleslady. She turns back and says she doesn't believe me (mothers try to sell the idea that they understand but do they really?).

I decide since she is so rude I'll just tell her anything! So I say, "Really I'm the President of the Cancer Prevention Society!" Now I notice a friend beside me who is a therapist (healer). We walk outside together and join a group of women out there (outside the conventional). I begin to tell them that teenagers are different now than they were when we were young.

At the end of the dream came her answer. To prevent a cancerous growth in that relationship, she should treat her daughter differently. That same night she also had this dream.

I have a new goldfish in a bowl. I put in a lovely rock and think to myself, "Do fish in their natural habitat see rocks and use them for landmarks?" I realized that they don't need landmarks and only have to follow their own instincts.

She too, like every mother, has golden (valuable) instinctual guides that she can follow in her emotional journeys.

Another lucky little girl, about seven years old, had a mother who came to one of our adult education dream study classes. Remember, we didn't need any psychologist to figure this out because it fit the situation in her home.

> I was in the house and a neighbor boy came running in to tell me my little girl had fallen off her bike (things were off balance for her daughter!).
>
> I ran out to see her, she was bruised and her eyes were rolling! I went into the house for an ice pack but I overfilled it (the mother's reaction was too cold).
>
> My husband had put our daughter on the stairs (stairs are a series of repeated steps—a big clue to this situation). He is yelling at her, "Why didn't you look what you were doing?" My husband's face fades and becomes my father's face. My daughter's face fades and becomes my sister's face (shows that like her father in the past, her husband is too harsh). We are going to take our daughter to the hospital because her eyes are rolling!

When she woke up, immediately the mother remembered an incident from her childhood. She had been left in charge of her sister and because of her being negligent, the sister had injured her eyes and had to be taken to the hospital.

If she continued to be cold and neglect the father/daughter and mother/daughter situation in her home, she would have a seriously injured daughter, emotionally speaking.

Another mother had this dream after a day of bitching at her children in a manner she agreed was shocking.

> My children had a pregnant mother dog

> with an electrical type name, I don't re-
> member what it was exactly. But I said her
> puppy's name could be Switch.

From the pregnant idea in that dream she entered
the next day reborn. She did Switch and for at least one
day she didn't 'dog' (bitch at) her kids.

Besides not 'bitching' too much, mothers shouldn't
'bug' their children too much. It could be deadly to the
relationship. I call this dream, "Snug as a Bug in a
Rug", or "Don't Make the Same Mistake Twice."

This mother had two daughters. The older one had
left home recently due to the mother's bugging her too
much about a lot of things — clothes, etc.

> The older daughter had sent home a
> carton of stuff to her sister. Mother and
> younger daughter were taking the stuff
> out. They took out the older daughter's
> throw rug and shook it. Much dirt came
> out and also a tiny but deadly bug.
> The mother called the father and he
> came and smashed the bug. The mother
> woke feeling depressed and frightened.

A warning. The same deadly bugging is now 'getting
to' this daughter, too. She needed to get the father to
help her, or be more accepting of the daughter as he is.
Second dream the same night:

> Younger daughter was younger still and
> going off to school. The father was going
> to drive her to school and the mother
> hugged and kissed her goodbye. The fam-
> ily felt close.
> The mother is talking to other women

and saying that children are different nowadays.

The suggested action: get back the family closeness with the father's help and be understanding of today's teenagers. Oftentimes fathers are more sensible, less emotional, about the children.

> In another dream she walked into her son's room and saw a large unusual bug on the wall between his room and her room. It was flesh colored. I went to get his father to come and look at it. When he got there the bug was gone.

The mother is bugged by her son. It is only a surface (flesh colored) behavior. But it is a barrier (wall) between them. The father just can't see it. The little things don't bug father at all.

This mother was really pushing it too far. She was badly tarnishing what had been a truly golden relationship.

> We are in a room where everything, walls, floor, furniture is burnished gold.
>
> I was mad at my two sons and wanted them to say they were sorry about something.
>
> I pressed one's thumb and he apologized.
>
> I pressed the other one's thumb and I was hurting him terribly. He said, "I love you" but wouldn't say, "I'm sorry." I wondered how he could stand so much pain.

I woke up feeling he must hurt terribly and hoping I'd have enough sense to accept "I love you" and not press for "I'm sorry."

This mother and son had 'gone round' that afternoon and in the evening had a really bad fight. She refused to lend her car to him and he had to walk to a friend's house. That night she dreamed:

> I had sent my son to the dentist because his lower teeth were crowded and grew in two rows. The dentist pulled several. Now his teeth were sort of sparse.

Since teeth are often symbolic of our speech, this mother knew the dream meant she had overdone it. His speech had been crooked it's true. But now too much speech, power of expression, had been taken away!

Another mother, another dream.

> Son came into our bedroom while I was biting father's ear. He wanted some change — nickels, dimes, quarters — *change*, not folding money.
>
> I was upset. Then I saw my son like he was about nine years old and I gave him a big hug and remembered my freckle-faced darling.

Mom was biting father's ear! She complained to father about the son even though she's sorry afterward because father goes to extremes. Son wants a change — back to when mom loved him as her freckle-faced darling!

Another mother got this "dream glimpse" of her son's mental and emotional state.

> Son was a boy of about 10 or 12. Father telling him he was stupid, etc. Son cried

> and cringed. Mom held him and he changed
> to present age (19 years), crying and saying,
> "Is it really time to grow up and be a
> man?" Mom hugged him tight and said,
> "Yes, it is time, but don't be afraid." He
> felt better.

Though this was a dream of the mother's, she felt it so strongly she described it as an experience. It seemed to have an improving effect in the mother/son relationship as if it had in some way acted on his consciousness also.

Another mother had one son she was particularly concerned about and one she was confident of and took for granted. This dream alerted her on his behalf.

> The family was on vacation (she's not on
> the job). Their hotel room was on the *second
> floor*. Her son, 'For Granted,' came into
> the parent's sleeping room and asked if he
> could go out and get a donut (sounds like
> "do not"). Parents sleepily said okay. He
> headed for the French windows of their
> room, thinking it was a door and forgetting
> they were on the second floor.
> Mother yelled, "Don't go out there," but
> it was too late. She ran to the window and
> saw him lying in a ball on the ground,
> moaning. In a flash she ran down the stairs
> calling for husband to follow and for the
> *house physician*. She woke flooded with
> anxiety for the son she usually took for
> granted.

In a couple of days this son had an experience with a

friend that left him stunned, hurt, confused and bitterly disappointed. He was suffering severe mental/emotional anguish. Being used to sleepy parents who took him for granted, he didn't say much at first. But the mother had been alerted by the dream and noticed his withdrawn attitude. She questioned him and took time to talk with her son. It helped him to grow and learn understanding from the hurtful experience, and brought them much closer together.

This mother is getting information from her dreams about the do-it-yourself sex education classes being held by her son's friends. This led her to initiate subtle but educational conversations of her own and to encourage her son to be more active in sports and spend his time with other companions.

> My neighbor's son, Bill, and his girl had been out until 5:00 A.M. and were locked out. Joe, my son, let them in our house and was feeding them jam tarts. I made the other youngsters leave. They piled into a long red car (male sex symbol) and started dizzily (uncontrolled) down the street. Bill was driving the girl's car but thought he was driving his dad's car (thinks he's big stuff). He kept talking to his girl and not looking where he was going. Not only that— he was driving from the wrong side of the car. Nearly hit a little kid.

Dreams as family counselor also alert receptive fathers to their roles in parent/child relationships. Here's an example from the life of Mr. Knight.

> My wife was leaving for work and I was staying home. I asked if she wanted me to clean the house.
>
> She said, "Great." As she walked *upstairs,* a drop of hot water hit her face and she realized the ceiling was leaking. I, following her upstairs, had the same experience. We knew it was because our oldest boy had been taking such long showers in such *hot water.* She left for work and I was going to clean up the bathroom and stop the leak.

This dream came at the beginning of their son's "senioritis" when he was getting into hot water with the school authorities. The dream made the dad aware that he was going to have to take a more active part in straightening out the boy. A couple of days later the school called and for a change he went and talked to the counselor instead of leaving it up to his wife.

This dream alerted 'Mr. Boa' that his constriction of the family was leading them toward a big letdown.

> I took the family to live on a mountainside where the houses around were being constructed. The ground was loose and I felt the potentiality of a landslide.
>
> My wife asked what the family was to eat. I told her I had only brought "harm and cheese."

'Mr. Boa' associated cheese as a food which binds and constipates. As he said, "The problem here is my constriction of my sons. It is harmful. Hence the pronouncing of ham as 'harm.' Also, I had led them to loose, dangerous ground. However, there is a hopeful note: We are in a construction site, not a finished tract. Knowing all this, I can improve the family relationships."

Divorce often figures importantly in parent/child relationships. A dream reminded this mother not to be so concerned with her own feelings that she neglects her children.

> I saw an Oriental woman leading my children through a tangled patch of woods.

She needed to orient herself to be a guide for the children through this time of confusion.

Mrs. Angel was very concerned about the treatment being given her husband's son, Tommy. Tommy, nine years old, was living with his natural mother and a stepfather. They didn't pay much attention to Tommy. Mrs. Angel and Tommy's father were beginning to talk about trying to get custody of Tommy. These are two of her dreams at that time.

> My husband and I were in a small bar, but not the usual type bar. This bar was like someone's living room. (Mr. Angel was a lawyer, member of 'the bar'). I don't remember the room having a window but since we were on the side of a hill, we could see down the hill and look at the different apartment houses below us. As we looked out, a man came to the balcony of his apartment and sat on the rail with his feet on the outside. He had a boy about Tommy's age with him and it appeared he was trying to throw him over the side. We decided to go see what was happening and went to the apartment house. We only

got to the parking lot and noticed the man had gone back inside and was coming down the stairs. We didn't want him to notice us so we pretended to be working on a car that was nearby. After the man passed, we decided it was over and we went back to the bar. Just as we settled down, the man returned to the balcony and did the same thing again. This time we ran down the hill to see what was the matter and again the man had gone back into his apartment.

This dream seemed to support their waking feeling that the stepfather would like to get rid of Tommy. But what about their chances of getting custody and helping Tommy? In this next dream, just visualize the trailer as a symbol for Tommy. It looks like he may soon be trailing or traveling along with them. Perhaps it's a golden opportunity.

My husband and I bought a small trailer with a dome top. It was terribly dirty, but with lots of work we got it sparkling. The trailer was drafty, especially the dome top, and we bought some raincoats lined with a maroon and gold cotton material which we attached to the top. We had put gold carpeting down and made the trailer quite comfortable.

The lady who originally owned the trailer before was in the dream, but I don't remember her participating. My brother and sister-in-law came to see the trailer and I noticed there was a gold pickup truck attached to the trailer which was also painted gold.

Sibling rivalry or sometimes revelry also figures in family dreaming. These dreams are from the life of a young boy guiding him in his relationship to his older brothers.

> 1. I have a snake in a bottle. Brother A (who pushes me around all the time) comes in and pushes me. I drop the bottle. The venomous snake gets out and bites me!

If he keeps his venomous feelings bottled up, his brother may push him too far and he will get bitten. It was not big brother who got hurt. The important thing in most relationships is how we react, they can't hurt us if we don't let them.

Fortunately, the boy told his mother about the dream and she was able, being a student of dreams, to help him understand that. She talked to both boys about brotherly love. Remarkably, the older boy improved his behavior toward his brother considerably.

Brother B is the middle boy whom the younger one followed around like a puppy dog.

> 2. Me and Brother B and his friends are at a convention. We all get up to make a protest march out of the convention meeting. We cause quite a disturbance. When we get outside there is a riot due to other teenage demonstrators.

If you walk out on the conventional, established values just following your brother's lead, you may get into trouble. They did, and got into trouble. There was quite a disturbance.

Younger sisters often idolize their older brothers. Debbie pined for her older brother and seriously considered following him to a college of his choice. She dreamed this about two weeks before going from California to visit him there.

> I dreamed I went to visit my brother in Oregon. I drove there for the day. I went to his college. A man pointed to his dorm. It was a pine tree. I climbed up the wood steps. His room was on the fifth floor; I think Room 503 (that's his area code). His room was in a paper sack. He said he'd be out in a minute. I was really disappointed because his room was so small and junky.

Subconsciously she had probably been aware of various shortcomings, but this dream prepared her to bring them to conscious awareness. She decided after seeing him that 'his bag' was really not so great. This was really quite important to her. It helped her decide that college might be 'his bag' but it was not for her. She happily decided to go to secretarial school, a better personal choice for her.

Sometimes the whole fam-damily gets involved. In the case of Mr. and Mrs. Nice that was their problem. They never got away by themselves—until after this dream! She tells it this way:

> I dreamed my husband and I were in a cozy cabin at Lake Tahoe. We had come there for a vacation—just the two of us. We were getting quite intimate but I felt very nervous. I kept feeling as if people

> were outside in the dark spying on us through the windows. Just when we were really getting into the lovemaking—Surprise! Scads of friends and relatives came bursting into the room.

"That dream really made me face up to how much I was resenting so much friend and family contact!" Mr. and Mrs. Nice later reported they really enjoyed their much needed, intimate vacation for two.

On the other hand, Tonya was in danger of neglecting some of the close family ties built up during her childhood. As often happens, a dream came in advance of the crisis time. Because she recorded her dreams, she was alert enough to avert a minor disaster. Her two dreams:

> I'm back at the vacation home where I spent so many happy summers and holidays with my cousins. Cousin Leticia and Cousin Sonia are there. I go into a back room and flip a switch. When I come back to the front room, it is on fire. Somehow my flipping the switch started the fire. I'm very sorry, I hadn't realized that flipping this switch would start a fire.

Second dream:

> I'm again back at the vacation home. This time I'm dressing for Cousin Leticia's wedding. But I'm late and everyone else has already left for the church. I got to the church just in time for the reception.

Soon after these dreams she received an invitation to

her Cousin Leticia's home for a holiday. She accepted, then later decided to go elsewhere. After telling Leticia about the *switch* in her plans she remembered the dreams. Rather than cause a family problem, she wisely decided to go to both places. Cousin Sonia told her how upset they had been when she first switched them off (fire often symbolizes ire). But their reception of her when she did arrive late was acceptable.

Sometimes cousins are not a good influence; each case must be judged individually according to the particular life situation. Ruth, David's mother, was alerted to the bad influence of her sister-in-law's son, Ronnie. Not that Ronnie could help it, he is a hyperactive child but his parents refuse to get professional help for him. However, Ruth's first concern should be for the needs of her son, David. The sister-in-law often wanted to take David home to play with Ronnie. She let Ronnie be so wild he had no friends so she began picking up his younger cousin, David. One day soon after this arrangement began, Ruth had this dream, probably a reaction to David's increasingly wild behavior.

> David is driving me in my car. He is taking me shopping (going to get something needed — his need). As we drive away, I notice there are people around so I go back to lock up our house (keep other people out!).
>
> As David drives I keep saying, "Slow and easy, slow and easy" (that is exactly what he needs). Next, we are at Ronnie's house; his mother, June is chasing around with a club in her hand. A large black rabbit and

> some other animals are loose in her house. Ronnie is watching with a sly grin on his face. He had stolen these animals from the 5-and-10 cent store and then let them loose. June is frantically trying to round them up. I say, "That's what happens when you don't look!"

How clever of little five year old David to drive his mother over there! Even though she didn't look in waking life, her dream mind made her see. "Pretty wild," huh?

I have no friends and no enemies — only teachers!

> I dreamed I went into a jewelry store to pick up a diamond ring (engagement ring). I put it on my finger and hurried out. Then I noticed the ring wasn't made the way I'd ordered it. The diamond was in a rectangular shape but mounted to fit crosswise on the finger instead of lengthwise. Also, the diamond was set flush with the mounting so no light could get in under it and there was no beautiful light refraction. I felt disgusted — the jeweler should have known better.

Something this dreamer was engaged in was not turning out well. It could have been a jewel of an experience but the other party involved bungled the set-up. She knew which friend it was!

'Mrs. Kind' had this dream showing her the friendly thing to do.

> We were at the women's club meeting. 'Mrs. Overbearing' was wearing a puffed

up bra and a black and white lacy blouse. She kept standing between 'Mrs. Meek' and the rest of the women. I reached over and deflated 'Mrs. Overbearing's' left boob. Felt glad because it showed her obviously false front. 'Mrs. Overbearing' turned and stormed out and 'Mrs. Meek' smiled at the group. She seemed to sort of glow.

'Mrs. Kind' made a concerted effort thereafter to keep 'Mrs. Overbearing' from dominating 'Mrs. Meek'. 'Mrs. Meek', encouraged by this, slowly began to contribute to the group discussion and proved to be a great joy.

Faye tells this dream. "A friend who was frivolous and a big waste of time had just gotten a new dress outfit in lime and white. She drove a Camaro. We had just become friends and she wanted to practically possess me. My dream:

I am in a factory area (work on this). A lime and white Camaro is going around on a display rotator (this gal goes round and round getting nowhere). A woman who had recently had an accident in a Camaro said, "Those Camaros are the stupidest, most frivolous cars I've ever seen."

I drove away in some different kind of car with my sister. In a room we found a very, very old woman (her mature self). We gave her a candy Easter egg (sweet; resurrection; new life) on a white plate (white — pure; plate — circle, well-rounded). It turned out the egg was meat. The old woman was so grateful she insisted on giving me a kiss.

The dream seemed to advise—drive away from the frivolous, non-religious girl and take good food to mature self (feed on those things I find most valuable) and she will embrace you (which I feel can help me to be pure and whole (integrated personality)."

Joann and Sue are close friends. When Sue was having a problem and needed a friend to talk to, Joann had this dream.

> I go into an *appliance* store. I've come to *sue* them! I am waiting to talk to the service/*repair* manager.

Joann was a willing sounding board while *Sue* discovered the need to *apply* herself if she expected to manage the *repair* of her problem.

We all have a friendly, willing sounding board in our dreams. Listen, there's a lot more being said in your sleep than just "Snore, snore!"

Chapter 6

Checks and Balances

To save ourselves we must face
ourselves; though not irration-
ally if reason is transcended.
　　　　　　— George R. Mead
　　　　　　Fragments of a Faith Forgotten

> I'm on a boat going to Europe for a
> vacation (escape, change). We are far out
> at sea (he's all at sea in his life). As I look at
> America the land looks a very pale green.
> As I look forward, toward Europe, the
> grass looks brilliant green. Soon we dock in
> Europe and the grass is the same pale green
> I saw as I looked back. ('The grass looks
> greener on the other side' — but it isn't!) I
> feel disappointed and angry!

Hal had gone to three colleges before finally gradu-
ating. He continually changed jobs and girlfriends and
had never married. At forty-two he felt real disappoint-
ment and bitterness in his lonely life. This dream pic-
turing his life dilemma came at a time when he was
contemplating another job change.

People often seem to keep meeting the same type of problem or situation over and over again. This is sometimes termed their life dilemma and will be pictured in their dreams. Hal's life dilemma or repeated experience was that 'the grass always looked greener on the other side of the fence.' When situations began to require real commitment he always moved on, but he never got any real satisfaction from anything either.

According to Maria Mahoney in *The Meaning in Dreams and Dreaming*, "Far from being 'sleep protecting' as the Freudians say, the unconscious launches a dream to wake up a dreamer to some aspect of his conscious life or personal attitude about which he is sound asleep!" The conscious, subconscious and superconscious minds make up a system of checks and balances such as the governmental system of the United States. Sometimes the functioning is painful just as the country experienced with President Nixon and the Watergate incident. Edgar Cayce said that the alternative to recalling and interpreting dreams is not always pleasant. Persons cannot expect to drift forever. Said Cayce:

> . . . that which is constantly associated in the mental visioning in the imaginative forces, that which is constantly associated with the senses of the body, that will it develop toward . . . There are *no* individuals who haven't at *some time* been warned as respecting that that may arise in their daily or physical experience!
>
> *Cayce Reading 5754-3*

The crisis may be physical, occupational, marital or other. Judy had been raised in a family where communication was a severe problem. She had learned *not* to express her thoughts and feelings to those close to her. Naturally, this had brought about a crisis in her marriage. She was uncommunicative and felt lonely and blocked off. This dream, which states the situation so clearly, could be called a spotlight dream.

> I'm in a lonely building outside of town. A young girl is being held captive by her family (this is Judy under the influence of her parents and the lack of communication in the home of her childhood). No one in this dream family will talk to anyone, not even each other. This girl has dirty hair (poor thinking). Also, her elimination system is all blocked up (Judy can't talk and get things out of her system). The girl has a green knob on her throat. I am able to turn it a very little bit. I know that if it can be loosened to turn freely her elimination system will be okay, she will be unblocked. I am going to put her in my car and take her to town. I hope to find someone there who can fix the knob and get her unblocked.

Towns are places of group activity. By bringing Judy to the dream group and working on her communication problem, she made a lot of growth and brought healing to the marriage situation. Green is often the color of growth and healing.

Later, Judy had this dream which shows how much progress she has made and promises rewards in the marriage relationship.

I, Judy, am coming home to my parents' home after just having had a frizzy permanent wave cut off of my hair (she has gotten rid of this unattractive habitual way of thinking). At their house I'm trying to find the stuff to wash and set my hair. I finally get it washed. I go into my mother, she is very senile (almost died out). I ask to borrow her hair setting lotion. She says, "If you use it you won't be able to tell if the permanent wave (thinking habit) is really all cut off!"

Next, I go to a bedroom attached to my parents' home (Judy's marriage). I help Cindy, a very morose and uncommunicative girl, move out. Then I begin helping Carol, a loving and expressive girlfriend, move in. Now I notice that my shorter hair is dry. I never did get my mother's setting lotion. The old kinky wave in my hair is all cut off.

Next, I am at a sink. Some pencils (phallic symbols point to the relationship with her husband) had gone down the drain! A friendly man is in the water under the sink. He pushes the pencils up to me, soon I have all of the old pencils back. He also pushes up some nice new pencils. One of the new pencils is very special, it is gold and 'really sharp'! I appreciate his efforts on my behalf.

The improvement in her personality, moving out 'Morose Cindy' and moving in 'Expressive Carol' is solving her marriage crisis. This part of Judy's dream resembles a typical dream pattern used to point out personality problems. Often the dreamer and Person A are doing some work for Person B. In this pattern, Person B represents a bad trait which the dreamer is beginning to develop or also has. Person A represents the opposite good trait which the dreamer should use to solve the problem. Here is an example of this pattern as it appeared in one father's dream.

> Mr. A was helping me clean out Mr. B's garage. We took a lot of trash to the dump.

Mr. B was very critical of his family, he was known for heaping trashy remarks on his wife and children. The dreamer had begun to do the same, especially as his children became older. Mr. A was patient and accepting of his children, their limitations and the ways of the new generation. The dream is saying, let the accepting ways of Mr. A help you clean out the trash of the way you've been acting like Mr. B.

Here is a wife's dream illustrating the same pattern.

> Mrs. A was helping me do Mrs. B's laundry. My fuzzy slippers were in amongst the laundry. We used All detergent.

Mrs. B was noted for interfering in her husband's life, even his business. This had led to her separation from him. Mrs. A was known for trusting her husband and advising other wives to stay out of the husband's business affairs. The dreamer had a fuzzy understanding of something her husband was about to embark on. They had argued about it during the day before her dream. Clearly she should be trusting like Mrs. A, not interfering like Mrs. B. She should get it All cleaned up!

Sometimes the dream message is less explicit, merely saying—Grow up! If you get one of these, look at what you did that day; were you childish about something? A young mother had this dream which came right out with it.

> I am walking to class somewhere (going to learn a lesson). I am wearing bobby socks with high-heeled shoes. I realize I look ridiculous but there is some reason for this combination. (She had acted childish in her grownup role.) Tom Kennedy, leader of the T.V. program titled, "The Split-Second Show", appeared and said, "It is time for you to make a change from a little girl to a woman." I took off the bobby socks!

Tom had been out of high school for three years and still hadn't held a steady job or entered a consistent course of study. He and his friends just drifted, doing as little as possible. His dreams say, "Get going!"

> I, Tom, am at a greenhouse (greenhouses are places of planned, cultivated growth). The greenhouse is on the corner of Valley Street (he is at a low point, valley, but it is also at a turning point or crossroad, corner).
>
> I go inside and find my parents with a gypsy (Tom's association to gypsy was a traveling person). They are at a table loaded with delicious looking fresh fruits. They all say, "Come on and eat."

In other words, Tom, you're at a turning point. Start

planning for growth and cultivating your talents. Get going and eat of the fruits of life. Finally, Tom entered a vocational training course in February 1974. Then he had this dream.

> I am flying about five hundred feet above the ground. I look down and see my friends below me. It feels good. Then I go in the house and see the *National Enquirer* newspaper with large headlines, PREDICTIONS FOR 1974.

The dream seems to predict that he will get himself off the ground in 1974 and rise above his friends. After finishing the course he is ready for the first day on his new job. He dreams:

> A voice says, "On your mark! Get set!" Then the alarm clock wakes me up to "go!"

Shakespeare's admonitions "Know thyself" and "To thine own self be true" are still good advice. Mrs. Blake had been divorced for eleven years. A friend who was just going through divorce asked Mrs. Blake one day, "Are you bitter about the way your husband deserted you to raise your children and all that?" Mrs. Blake said, "No." Then her dream that night gave her a check on that bit of self-knowledge.

> My husband and I are selling our house (back to the time of the breakup). I had washed down the walls (she cleansed the barriers). I decided to repaint and to do it during the week while the children would be in school, (she is putting a new appearance on the consciousness represented by

that old family home now that her children are grown and out of the nest). This is a good time to freshen up. I decide to paint the hallway (passage of time), top half white and bottom half green (a balance of two good colors).

I have bought extra paint for my new home, too. My sister (another way of life) will help me paint my new home.

Next, company is arriving at my new home. My son carries in a big turkey (reminder of thanks giving). We have a white tablecloth and the table is loaded with good food. I get out my pretty plates which have been packed away (she has good facilities for serving).

On a side table I am slicing cakes and I find some ants crawling over here (there are a few irritating side effects in the dessert area; also, the cake could represent her husband as he had been a baker). Now I see a dirigible with my husband and children and a load of baked goods. It plunges into a lake (the lake would be her emotional reservoir where this experience now rests).

Mrs. Blake had a second dream that night. It gives a further assessment of how she really feels about the desertion and divorce experience.

I'm in my front yard (outer consciousness) watching bombs explode in the distance. Great flames go up from the earth. The bombs seem to be getting nearer and a tidal wave is coming. My dog (domesticated instincts) is nonchalant and unaffected. I turn to run toward my backyard

> (inner consciousness). When I turn back to look (as she had that day) there are no flames and no tidal wave! (It really is over for her, she no longer has emotional turmoils from that distant bomb drop.)

Mrs. Blake was right, even in her backyard (the back of her mind) she is not bitter!

This divorcee, Ms. Mayo, does not know herself. She is making the same mistake that she projects on the American male. She is judging her book by its cover and has rejected her own inner beauty. Her outer life situation shows this as well as her dream. She is very concerned and preoccupied with a strenuous diet and her outer appearance. These she feels are the keys to attracting a man into her life. Her dream seems to say she has a really beautiful woman within.

> I see a foreign dumpy looking woman. She says to me, "American men's attitude toward women is missing so much. They want a beautiful woman. In me they only see the dumpy and the fat stomach, they miss so much!" She seemed quite angry. As I watched she changed to a glowing beautiful woman with her hands out to me.

If Ms. Mayo had needed the diet it would have been different but she already was outwardly attractive. But men actually are more attracted to the projection of inner beauty and confidence.

High school graduation is naturally a time to take a good look at one's self. But youth has problems deciding how much family tradition to continue and which peer group attitudes are really attractive. Susan's dreams show her that her family foundation is clear and is ready to go with her to meet the lessons of adult life. But she is not clear about her own choices.

> 1. I have to move to a different state (beyond high school) with my family. All of a sudden the fact really hit me and I only have half an hour to say goodbye to all my friends. I rush around to see everyone, we are crying and hugging each other. I was upset because I knew I would really miss all my friends (rehearsal for the coming experience also symbolic of the break with the relative ease of student life).
>
> When I get back to my house my family is standing there waiting for us. They are all ready to go.
>
> 2. I am in my room in front of two mirrors trying on clothes (attitudes). I am getting ready to go to a new school (the school of adult life). Some of the clothes I try on I don't own in real life. I am in a big hurry and am throwing clothes all over the place. The room was rather dark. I can see from the waist down okay (her foundation) but I can't see very well from the waist up. I keep asking my best friend (the best of the peer group), "Do I look okay, does this color look good on me?" I am very concerned with my appearance.

Tessie, another high school girl, is being told not to turn her back on all of the values of the past.

> All of my friends and I are in a small cabin (the consciousness, cabin, of the peer group is small). I get into my girlfriend's

car and she drives away (Tessie is not in the
driver's seat of her life). My girlfriend hits
another car but just drives away like it was
no big thing (hit and run attitude of the
peer group). We go into an antique shop
and browse around for a while. We see
many valuable old things. Then we go
back to the cabin (peer group consciousness).

The cabin is crawling with cockroaches.
They are flying and jumping everywhere.
I am deathly afraid. One jumped on my
bed so I wouldn't sleep there anymore.

After getting a look at the old fashioned values she
can see how creepy the values of her friends are. They
bug her. The idea here that Tessie is not in the driver's
seat is like that old fashioned idea, "To thine own self
be true." She is now awake to the situation. She won't
sleep there anymore.

With young people, the choice of attitude toward sex
is an important area of concern. The young men and
the peer group seem to favor pre-marital lovemaking.
The 'wise-old woman' feminine instinct seems to favor
girls holding on to their feminine purity. One young
girl was having a tug-of-war in her consciousness. She
stated that she had been 'on the brink' with her boyfriend several times. Her dream:

My boyfriend is a member of a group or
cult (peer ideas) and wants me to join. He
takes me to "The Place." I have to open
large wooden (wouldn't) doors (female sex
symbol).

We go down dark stairs. Scattered old
dead people on both sides (murderous to

the old value). Down a long, narrow, dark passage. At the end we see a group and the Devil; he smiles. I am scared and run away. The group yells at me.

My boyfriend is taking me back there again. I say, "This time I'm going through with it." I see the Devil, he smiles. They say she has to give up a part of her body to join (virginity). My eye (I) tooth falls out in my hand; then *all* of my teeth fall out (loss of something irreplaceable and valuable). They say, "Give us your teeth." I get mad and throw my teeth at them. Each one puts one of my teeth around their neck on a string. The Devil starts to grow and has shiny clothes. I go through the Devil and to an old primitive man, large and dark. He has one of my teeth on his forehead (foreskin).

So far, the dream says, "If you go through with this devilish, primitive action, you will lose an important part of your self-image, something valuable and irreplaceable.

The vice mayor (leader in charge of vice) appears with a newspaper clipping (current message). There is a photograph of a city councilman (her inner counsel) and his family. I am ordered to kill the councilman and my boyfriend is to kill one of his sons (they would both be guilty of killing their better values). I say, "I won't, I can't!!" The cultists chase me.

I come to an old woman who says that if I do what I have to I can have my choice of

her many women's necklaces. I choose a
white shell necklace (white — purity; shells
— ancient valuables; circular necklace —
wholeness). I go to a cliff where I know I
must jump off and die.

She will have to deny her lower self if she is to receive
the valuable and beautiful gift from the wise old
woman (the instinct to preserve her feminine purity).

Being true to one's self may mean cutting the apron
strings and disappointing your parents. It may mean
disagreeing with your current set of friends or your
spouse, but we should have the courage of our own
convictions. I call this next dream 'Emancipation Proc-
lamation!' The dreamer was in her early twenties.

I was in the front yard of my parent's
home with my brother. It was nighttime.
I looked at the sky above our house (family
thinking); I saw strange things happening.
Brilliant colored lights appearing from nowhere, making enormous light patterns
flashing on and off. They seemed to be
telling me something. It was so exciting
and beautiful I ran into the house to tell
my parents to come and see. They weren't
interested (parental indifference)! I won-
dered if maybe they weren't visible to my
parents (they 'can't see' the new thinking
patterns of her generation).

Then I was outside again but it was
daylight, (more light on the subject). Part
of the ivy was gone from the hill in front of
the house. I discovered that the ivy had
been covering some hidden steps (steps she

can now take). I followed the steps uphill
to a small cave. In the cave (her unconscious mind) I found a rare photograph of
Abraham Lincoln reproduced to poster
size (a posted notice of freedom). On the
poster was a black spider (fear). I asked my
brother to kill it for me and he did (her
brother is older and has already cut the
apron strings as an example to her). I took
the poster and decided to hang it up in my
apartment (a place apart). I woke up feeling excited about the lights.

Another college girl got the message symbolized as
falling out of the family tree.

We are having a family picnic; there is
a tree in the middle. I am on one side of
the tree and the rest of the family is all on
the other side. My sister's former husband
was in the tree and fell out flat on his face,
dead. I felt great sympathy for him and
ran to his side.

Her brother-in-law had been a bit of a radical, a
free-soul. Her father was far too conservative to accept
this and this broke up that marriage. Since the dreamer's sympathies are with the brother-in-law, she is quite
modern too; she can expect somewhat the same fate,
falling out of the family tree; she ran in that direction.

How about wives' liberation? Mrs. Bright dreamed
this.

My husband came to me and asked me
where his sunglasses were. I said, "I don't
know." He became quite angry. I resented

> his anger. I told him, "I don't think it is my
> responsibility to keep track of your sun-
> glasses."

Questioning revealed that her husband took a very dim view of everything (seeing the world through dark glasses). She didn't want to be on that track with him.

Of course, we should be willing to let others be true to themselves. A new bride dreamed about that side of the coin.

> I am trying to drive my husband's car,
> but I can't control it!

The usual cycle of development has a place for being a child, a lover and a parent. These expressions seek outlets. Sometimes a person gets too stuck in one level. That was Linda, she got stuck at the little girl stage. Linda had been a very pretty and very 'good little girl.' With her long black curls and ruffled dresses, she had received a great deal of attention from doting adults. When she came to the dream workshop, she was thirty-nine years old but she still wore long black curls and a ruffled, fluffy dress. Linda had once been married but was now a divorcee of several years. Her body language and appearance gave clues borne out by discussion. Her marriage and dating relationships failed because she expected to be treated like a beautiful child. She never matured enough to relate to a man in the supportive role of a lover. Therefore, she had never become a mother. For several years she had been greatly troubled by this recurring dream.

> I am in my apartment. I feel compelled
> to go to the windows. Each time I open one
> I find a blank wall. I know there should be
> something very valuable, something pre-
> cious behind the windows or doors. I begin
> frantically rushing from one to another but
> always I find blank walls. It seems that
> there is no way out of my apartment (place
> of aloneness). I usually wake up crying.

Linda had a very dramatic dialogue with the window
symbol from her dream. This revealed the agony of the
blank wall reality of her love life and her thwarted
mother instinct. One of the main themes of this workshop was the Senoi Indian Tribe practice of making
the messages useful to the tribe. From the group discussion, Linda got the idea to become a volunteer
helper to work with orphaned children. A socially
practical application of dream guidance.

Granny was another participant at the same workshop. However, she had gotten stuck at the other end
of the scale. Such a good responsible wife was she, that
her recreation times were all dictated and designed to
suit her husband's tastes. Also, much of her time was
taken up by babysitting with her grandchildren. Her
own 'little-girl-self' was sadly neglected. Hence, this
dream.

> I, Granny, am walking up a steep hill in
> the middle of a busy city (they keep her
> busy all right, wifing and mothering!). I go
> into a tall, dingy tenement building. I go
> into a flat. At first it seems that there is no
> one here. Then I see what I have come

for—a frightened little girl who has been abandoned here. I tell her I have come to take her to a picnic. She complains that she is afraid, she doesn't have a pretty dress, the sunlight will hurt her eyes. I am coaxing her to come out, I show her a big basket of fresh fruit. I wake up remembering I've seen this straggly little girl in other dreams.

In keeping with the theme of that workshop, to make practical group applications of the dream messages, we took Granny on a picnic. She didn't have to prepare a thing. It was great for her 'little-girl-self' and we all had a fun child-like picnic.

Another serious, hard working mother of several boys had this dream. In real life she had no daughter but every woman, psychologically, has a 'little-girl-self'.

I had a six year old daughter, she was wearing a bright dress of warm colors. She was mad at me and pouting because I had been neglecting her. She said I didn't love her because she wanted to ride a horse (symbol of libido energy) and I wouldn't let her. I said, "But I can't even ride that horse myself, I'm not strong enough; he's not all that tame. So, of course, you can't ride that horse."

I decided to get her a small-size, two-wheeler bicycle (keep the expression in balance). I went to look for one, second-hand. I didn't see any but saw several large black tricycles. I decided she wouldn't be satisfied with that. It was store closing time so I'd have to wait until tomorrow.

> I was letting my husband put her to bed.
> She was still sulking even though she knew
> I'd started to make an effort on her behalf.
> Husband was getting water for her musical
> cup.

(There would be more harmony and fun in the
marriage if she let the husband treat her like a little
girl sometimes.)

This one makes that common life situation very clear
for another overly conscientious grandmother.

> My granddaughter (her own *grand* 'child-
> like self') is sick in bed and I'm taking care
> of her. There is to be an important meeting
> of the 'Children's Aid Society' at noon
> (high-time). I'm not ready. I'm nervous
> because I don't have their food ready.

Fears within the personality structure also come
under the scrutiny of our dream consciousness. Jim was
a young white man who had some upsetting experiences while teaching in a black ghetto high school in
Los Angeles. After some time of working on his problem, he had this dream progress report.

> I am watching an all black movie and I
> liked it very much. The movie is being
> shown in a prison yard. The black director
> is against the wall. After the movie, I asked
> the director, "Was that the music of Calvin
> Jones?"
> "Yes," he answered, "it was."
> "Did you just discover him?" I asked.
> "Yes," answered the director.

> I had a very good feeling because I liked the movie, and the music of Calvin Jones. I was very pleased that I recognized the composer.

From the objective point of view, this dream indicates that Jim's feelings toward the Black People are vastly improved. From the subjective point of view it indicates that he is becoming more familiar with his hidden shadow side. Both of these meanings fit Jim, the person.

We met Ms. Mayo before, she was struggling with the problems of a recent divorce. There is fear of her new freedom. Her dream.

> I am an actress on Broadway. It is the opening of my new play (she is beginning a new role or stage in her life; it is broad, wide open). The opening was a success (good opportunity). There are two trained birds who have comic parts in the play. They get loose on the stage. I become frightened and swat them down (she pushed down her sense of humor). They refused to do their parts and now the play became a flop. It was the end of my acting career.

If Ms. Mayo doesn't enjoy her freedom (the birds on the loose), she will end up a flop. Let your sense of humor loose, don't be too serious. Humor is part of inner beauty and attractiveness.

The dreams in this chapter point to ways for the dreamers to improve their personality or character.

But what sets the valuation which decides what constitutes good character? There is a generally accepted standard which if not developed by the person leads to difficulties in relation to the people with whom one lives; and/or psychological repercussions within the person.

Concerning this factor in the system of the human psyche, Carl Jung said, "It should never be forgotten that morality was not brought down on tables of stone from Sinai and imposed on the people, but is a function of the human soul, as old as humanity itself. Morality is not imposed from outside; we have it in ourselves from the start—not the law, but our moral nature without which the *collective life* of human society would be impossible. That is why morality is found at all levels of society. It is the *instinctive* regulator of action which governs the collective life of the herd." Jung—*The Structure and Dynamics of Psyche,* pp. 243-244.

Be the problem large or small, common or individual, the psyche, through dreams, will send messages about it to the person's consciousness.

The ancient Chinese symbol of the Yin and Yang is a pictograph of the universal need for balancing opposites. Moderation in all things. The well-rounded, integrated person is able to draw from opposite possibilities and react to each life situation with the needed attribute:

logic or emotion
physical senses, facts or intuition

> reserve or boldness
> introversion or extraversion
> effort or relaxation
> etc.

"Wisdom begins when acquaintance with your own odd quirks equals your estimate of the overall queerness of everybody else!" said Maria Mahoney in *The Meaning in Dreams and Dreaming*.

> I met Mr. M. (a highly intellectual and logial person). He was coming from a lecture hall. Mr. M said to me, "I've been at a physics lecture about the 'Laws of Equilibrium.' It was an excellent lecture. There are three more in this series. You should go to the rest of them. The speaker is extremely good, her name is Joy Mills."

The dreamer, Fran, in this case was much like Mr. M, too serious. The dream is lecturing her to balance her life with some Joy. Another morning she woke up with this inversion of a famous quotation clearly on her mind.

> "A thing of joy is a beauty forever!"

Very appropriate for her and just as true as the original, "A thing of beauty is a joy forever."

Another dreamer who was living too much by logic and not enough by emotion had this spotlight dream.

> I'm in a lecture room. An old gypsy woman was telling about astral projection and auras. She stated that there are three

kinds of human personality—intellectual, natural and animal. She said that she could 'read' peoples' type by their vibrations. To demonstrate, she asked me to come up out of the audience. Then she said I was the intellectual type and needed to blend in more animal feelings.

Mr. M, who acted in Fran's dream as a symbol of an overly intellectual type, had this dream about his being on a 'head trip.'

My son (his approach to life as developed in childhood) is playing with another boy at a house. I go there to pick up my son. I have a feeling of danger. While waiting for him to put on his shoes and socks (understanding the childhood outlook), I sit on the floor in front of the sofa. The woman there gets behind me, (the woman behind him probably represents the influence of his mother). Before I know it she has stuck a long needle in the back of my head. I feel that I have floated to the top of the room against the far wall. After a few minutes I realize that I am back on the floor in front of this spooky woman. I realize my body had not really left the floor, it only seemed that way. *I'd been on a head trip!* I was furious that she would do that without asking and without warning. She was about to do it again but I grabbed her wrist and made her stick the needle into her own neck. There was no blood, just a clear liquid (a colorless person). I grabbed my son and ran from the house.

> About a block away we came to a church
> where some people were in the kitchen pre-
> paring to serve a pot luck dinner. I felt we
> were safe.

There is safety in getting into the spirit of life (church)
and taking 'pot luck'. Head trips are for bloodless,
colorless people.

Sometimes the balance between emotions and intellect is suppressed by the intellect. A common problem
with the generation who are now in their middle age.
Forty years old is not the best time to be reaching emotional maturity; the theme of our next dream example,
but better late than never. This long, but interesting,
dream was brought in by a male forty years old.

> I am visiting my parents in Maine (where
> they were in reality). I have come from my
> home in Florida (where my parents live in
> the winter, not at all where I live or ever
> have lived). I am in the Army (I once was).
>
> The day before I am to leave to return
> home, I somehow meet several young (20
> or 21 years old) girls who work for a large
> company (perhaps like Kodak, the biggest
> industry in Rochester where I live). They
> need to get to another city to the west of
> Rochester, perhaps Buffalo, though I am
> not clear on that. I offer to drive them.
> There are eight or nine girls, and it will be
> a tight fit in my parents' Volkswagen (I am
> the one who has owned a Volkswagen, my
> parents never).
>
> I borrow the car. No mention is made of
> when and how I should return it; I am

trusted (my parents have indeed always trusted me). I even have *all* the sets of keys.

I got to the factory where the girls work. It is very large and confusing, and I realize that I don't have enough knowledge about where to meet them. What I am doing begins to feel furtive.

I am looking for the girls in the basement cafeteria which is very shiny. There is a lot of chrome, polished brass and wrought iron in it. There is an open door from the cellar to the outside. There are brilliant shafts of sunshine streaming in through the cellar door and through the small windows high in the walls.

One of the girls (she reminds me of a girl who was on a tour of Europe I took in 1960) is sitting at the counter eating a sundae. Two more of the girls are there, too.

My wife appears looking very elegant (she actually wears jeans and peasant dresses most of the time). She has been shopping in a department store and has bought a very elegant and attractive black straw hat called a Brougham (in reality, a Brougham is a carriage with a folddown top) and when she wears it, though it covers only her head, her body diminishes and only her arms and legs are normal sized.

The girls and I part and agree to meet later in a "safer" place. They ask me not to reveal their plans to the FBI man who is lurking in the shadows. He wants to speak with me when they are gone. I agree. We part, and I leave the crowds of people in the cafeteria and walk through subterranean passages of the factory toward my parents' car.

It is night now. My plans are in shambles. I am walking across a bridge from the factory to the other side of a river. I walk on the left side of the bridge where there is a fence. The fence interferes with my walking since I straddle it (it is quite low), but it makes me very difficult to spot. Gradually, the fence grows higher and I am forced to jump down to a lower level of the bridge. This level of the bridge is crossed every few feet by an expandable gate. Most of them are open and pushed against the opposite side of the bridge.

The scene changes: My wife and I are sitting in my parents' car. She is sitting in the front in the passenger's seat and I am sitting behind her in the back. I have a small suitcase open on my lap. My parents have packed it for me. Among the clothes are many boxes of Fannie Farmer candy. Each box is a different extremely sweet, *sweet* variety. We have just bought some candy of our own, not knowing there is candy in the suitcase. My wife and I wrinkle our noses at each other because of the super sweetness of it all, but we break off large chunks of "blond fudge" (whatever that is!) and begin to eat it. This scene takes place in a busy, commercial street with much pedestrian and truck traffic. It is a beautiful midsummer day with bright sunlight, but very humid air. We seem to be waiting for the driver of the car to appear. Several

> questions are on my mind as I sit in the car waiting: Who is the driver? Where are the girls? Why isn't such a small car crowded-feeling? Are we on our way to the city to the west?

Since we use our personal cars as a means of getting around in our life, the dreamer's car represents his life and the movement in his life. In his dream it was his Volkswagen but owned by his parents, he had to borrow it! This dream then deals with an area of his life and personality which is still largely under the influence of his parents. We will look at the dream in parts and then sum it up.

> He is visiting his parents in Maine. He has come from his home in Florida (non-reality). He is in the Army.

Visiting or looking in on one of the main areas of parental influence. Since the dream represents him as having lived in Florida, which is really his parents' home away from him, it shows that this parental influence affects his life below the level of consciousness and even though they are far away. Being in the Army he is under the authority and discipline of his homeland (family) heritage.

> The day before he is to leave to return home.

It is about time to get away from this parental influence and go to his own way of life.

> He somehow meets several young girls about 20 or 21 years old.

Girls or female figures usually represent the feeling or emotional side of personality (male figures being the thinking or logical side). These girls are just reaching the age of maturity, 21. Here then is the crux of his dream. He is at a point in his life where he is meeting his own maturing emotional nature!! Your emotional sense and habits have been influenced by your parents' model. This is true for all people.

> These girls work for a large company, perhaps *Kodak*. They need to get to another city to the west of where he presently lives. He will take them there, but it will be a tight fit in his parents' Volkswagen!

These maturing emotions work for his total psyche, the large *developing company*. He is developing in the area of emotional maturity. Get the picture? But, fitting his ideas of mature emotions in with what he learned from his parents will be a tight squeeze. This might also indicate that it is in the area of relating to his parents that he needs to develop emotional maturity. These maturing emotions need to be carried beyond his present place, Rochester, to another city. Cities are centers of life activity, bring the developing emotional maturity into action!

> He borrows the car. No mention of returning it. He is trusted. He even has all the sets of keys.

He can take over his life and no need to concern himself with returning to the influence of his parents. His psyche tells him he can trust himself in this area.

He has all the necessary keys, that is, he has the know-how and ability to take control of his emotions in a developing mature way.

> He goes to the factory where the girls work. It is large and confusing and he doesn't know where to meet them. He feels furtive.

The factory, his subconscious and conscious, are not yet sure of meeting in the emotional area. He has hidden feelings but is beginning to feel them consciously. Bringing his hidden, unlived, subconscious feelings to the surface may be a little confusing.

> He is looking for the girls in the basement cafeteria, it is shiny. Lots of metal. There is a large door, brilliant shafts of sunlight enter through the door and windows.

In the basement, his subconsciousness below the surface, in the cafeteria, where there is food for thought, is the place to look for his maturing emotions. Metals may represent strength and durability. He has lots and it is well cared for! The door between his subconscious and his surface mind is open and he is getting lots of light on his basement factory!

> One of the girls, who had been touring with him in the past, is eating a sundae.

A sundae has two sweetnesses, the ice cream and the sauce. This type of emotionality, *too* sweet, sweet, sweet; has been traveling with him.

> His wife appears looking elegant (unlike her true normal appearance). She has bought an elegant black straw hat called a Brougham which is really a carriage. It covers her head but diminishes her body. The appendages remain normal.

Here his wife represents the emotional expression, female type, he chose to live with (she is standing for a part of his personality not her true literal self). This aspect of him appears to be elegant. He expresses only elegant emotions. It is just a dark carriage which is worn over the head (controls your thinking or is controlled by your thinking). This apparently elegant carriage which his emotional expression wears, really diminishes the body of him as a total person.

> The girls and he agree to meet later in a safer place. They do not want him to reveal their plans to the FBI agent. But he wants to talk to him! He agrees to talk to the FBI agent then goes back toward his parents' car.

His inner maturing emotions, which work for his total psyche, do not feel safe around his emotional expressions which he wears under the influence of his head and its elegant appearance. (He can put down this 'head rules the heart' influence and put it back up if he needs.)

His intellectual, investigative self, lurks in the shadows. His maturing emotions do not feel safe around his investigative agent. But he decides to talk to him. The emotions, girls, disappear and he wanders back through his subconscious (subterranean passages) to his parents' influence (their car). This is what he has been doing all his life, putting thinking (FBI) over emotions (girls). This chases the emotional response to life right out of sight.

> It is night now. His plans are a shambles. He is walking across a bridge from the factory to the other side of the river. He walks on the left side of the bridge where there is a fence. He straddles it, the fence interferes with his walking (progress). It gets higher and he is forced to jump down to a lower level of the bridge. At this level the bridge is crossed every few feet by an expandable gate. Most of them are open and pushed against the right side of the bridge.

In the darkness (below consciousness, in sleep), he blew the plan when he talked to the FBI (intellect, logic). The bridge is between factory, unconsciousness, and the other side, consciousness, flow of his life (river). If he straddles a fence (no progress), he must go down deeper on left side (unconscious, emotional side). At this level the gates of expansion are mostly open to him, being pushed against his intellectual side (the right).

> Wife and he are in his parents' car, she in passenger seat (going along with him), he in back seat. Small suitcase from parents (what they loaded him with or outfitted him with). Fannie Farmer *sweet, sweet* candy (parents' influence was to be too sweet and keep his emotions controlled 'under his hat').

> He nose (knows) it is too super sweet. His parents gave him blond candy, colorless, sweetness. It is fudge and 'Fudge!' is a slang expression of disappointment.
>
> He is waiting for a driver. Waiting to 'take off'; waiting for movement. Questions are on his mind.

The dream appears to be asking him to question himself regarding:

Who will be the driver of his life, emotionally?

Where are the girls? Where is his developing emotional maturity? (What is to be its status in his life?)

Why isn't such a small car crowded-feeling? (His life isn't fancy with more money and travel. That is, what he said he felt on the surface that he wanted.) But he has other important things such as a happy marriage, two children, an important job and he is developing emotional maturity.

The final question was, "Are we on our way to the city to the west?" It appears he can be, it is up to him. He may follow that American suggestion, "Go west young man, go west!" Make progress and expand.

The opposite problem would be a person who was too emotional in their reaction to life. Such a person was Myna. Her dreams told her that she needed to have masculinity, logic, to make herself well-rounded.

> She is in an apartment, a nice motel (temporary state of living). Her room is upstairs. Her sister (typified logic as the opposite approach to which Myna now lived) gave Myna a baby (new beginning) that

looked like the sister. Myna took the baby upstairs—into her consciousness and mental area. Holding the baby, she looked out the window and watched clouds blowing away. Behind the clouds was a circle (well-rounded). Behind the circle was a paradise and many men's faces (masculine expressions). Out of their mouths came doves.

For Myna, more masculine expression would be the mouthpiece (doves—peace) of paradise and wholeness.

So much for balancing intellect with emotions. Another balancing problem people have is with introvert and extrovert tendencies. Often in a family if one child is an introvert, brother or sister will be an extrovert, the opposite. Such a brother or sister who lives the opposite approach to life often will appear in dreams to symbolize that trait. For a person who is shy and introverted, it takes courage to express one's self more freely. More feeling for others is also needed to get an introvert to express more to others. This is one introvert's dream.

A man with a pickup truck had a load of copies of the first American flag (symbol of freedom at its inception). He was giving these to Boy Scouts who had a red badge ticket. The badges were 1½" x 4" rectangles of red felt material.

My sister walked up with one of the badges and got a flag. I asked her where she got the badge. She said, "You have to find them."

Some Boy Scouts were dropping packages of red badges but none were the right ones. The badge had to be a rectangular shape.

The sister, in real life an extrovert, had the ticket to freedom. It must be a rec-tangle. The dreamer frequently tangled up her life by being too shy and inhibited. But she had not yet found 'the red badge of courage' to express herself freely and wreck the tangles she created in her life.

A talkative extrovert who had a hard time being quiet and listening to others received this hint from her dreams.

> I saw Jackie, a quiet friend, wearing a red and white checked dress. It was lightweight satin. I was admiring the dress especially the red and white checks.

It says, check the balance of contrasting quiet and loud colors. It might be admirable if she sat in such a dress (attitude). Now again back to the opposite too cold and introverted a person.

> Dreamed I went into my bathroom (place of elimination). On the mirror was a sign about frozen vegetables. I had to remove the sign before I could see into the mirror. Then my sister (an extrovert) came up behind me and smiled at me in the mirror.

She needs to stop being so frozen and vegetating. She should reflect and project more like her sister who smiles on others. Finding a balance between too much out-goingness and too much introversion can be a problem.

> Mary, a very loud extravert, my sister, a balanced extravert, and myself, the very

quiet, introverted dreamer, have been sleeping on a sailboat in the outer harbor (I am almost 'at sea', out of touch with civilization). In the morning (awakening—becoming aware of the problem) the harbor officer unhooked one rope and we drifted further out to sea (the incident during the day that made her more aware of the problem).

My sister got on a different rope and slid easily to shore (she makes contact easily). I try to follow my sister but the rope is jerky (I make contact but it is difficult). The loud friend drifts further out to sea.

This extrovert feels lonely even in a group of people. She was a real manipulator of others but felt no closeness with them. Soon after joining a women's club she had this dream.

The car load of women pulls into a new town. We all get out and go into a restaurant. The group is sitting at one table and I am sitting alone at another table. I'm facing a wall and talking to myself. I get up to join the other women. I decided to go to the bathroom first. The clothes (attitude) I was wearing were such that I had to take them all the way off before I could go. I took them off, urinated, and felt relieved.

She has to change herself; take off the clothes, attitudes or personality, she now has on and get it out of her system—eliminate it. Then she will find relief from her cutoff feeling and move away from the barrier, wall, she is now facing.

Inner male/female duality is often symbolized by a hermaphroditic figure like this one.

The androgynous figure of ancient symbolism represents a person who has developed and balanced the masculine and feminine characteristics in their personality.

Every woman has aggressive, male characteristics potential in her psyche and some women behave with too much masculinity. Likewise, men have the potential to express in gentle feminine ways but hopefully not too much so.

This woman's animus, her masculine side, is calling on her to make contact.

> I was a foreigner living in Mazatlan, newly arrived. A man came to visit me but I was not home (not home to her male

side). I sent a regrets note and said if he'd
let me know a day ahead of time, I'd spend
the whole day visiting.

A native woman servant told me it was
okay for a woman to call on a man in
Mazatlan instead of waiting for him to
come to her.

Although the maleness in this woman is still dark
and unknown (foreign to her), this principle in her,
loves her and wants to join her in a life together.

I was engaged to marry a negro school
principal. The secretary was sending me
away, saying the engagement was off. I
said, "Why?" She said he would no longer
engage with whites. I knew this was a lie—
he wasn't prejudiced. She finally said it was
his mother's idea and she held the purse
strings. We had a big argument about
mixed marriages.

He came to pick me up. He was not
swayed by his mother, he would continue
to take care of me. He was very nice. I felt
real love and concern.

We walked out holding hands!

She later dreamed she was on a ship bargaining with
the captain to buy a large black slave his freedom.

Another woman whose masculine side was uncon-
trolled and caused her to be very domineering in her
marriage had these two dreams.

She was walking across a school play-
ground. A group of school boys, whose

> teacher was a butcher, were having batting practice with a large piece of steak. They were seeing who could hit it the highest. The dreamer was waiting for the teacher to come and take over the class. She waited an hour and the teacher did not come to give attention, instruction or discipline to the rowdy boys. The dreamer headed for the office to report the teacher.

Her masculine side is young, immature and rowdy. The stakes they are playing with and batting around are high (the marriage problem). She should get the instructor and disciplining agent on the job.

The same woman had another dream with the same message.

> I'm acting as a guest kindergarten teacher. I choose a group of all little boys to work with. We plan to start a project this week and finish it next week. Part one was to draw some animal pictures.
>
> The boys did excellent drawings. I remember a skunk (this male stinks), a pink (feminine color) dragon (fire breather!) and a lizard (creepy). Then the little boys went ahead and cut out the drawings without being told to. This *ruined the project by not following directions.*

This set of dreams is from another woman working on not being too masculine. She is shown when she began to have a masculine personality at junior high school age. Her second dream suggests a solution.

> I'm putting on my father's blue jeans.
> They don't fit too badly, not too long but
> a little baggy. I'm tucking in his T-shirt.
> Right sleeve is torn. It seems more too big
> than the pants. I'm supposed to be getting
> ready to go to school at my old junior high
> school (when the problem started). I de-
> cided my father's clothes (Attitudes) didn't
> look good!

Her second dream:

> I'm shopping in a fancy department
> store. I'm looking at new style dresses,
> fashioned for all occasions. Shorts suit in
> front and a long cape over the shoulders.
> Only ones seen in the dream were white
> and frilly like for a bride.

This suggests that she clothe herself in feminine
clothes (attitudes). Notice also that the pants are
shorts; she shouldn't be wearing the long pants in that
family.

If a woman has such a problem and watches her
dreams, she'll probably get a nice clear spotlight dream
like this.

> I met a dumpy looking woman, red hair
> hanging like a mop, overweight, faded
> housedress, slightly wrinkled skin.
> I was looking up at her like a small child.
> I was aware I was dreaming.
> I said, "Who are you?"
> She, "Your mother."
> Me, "But my mother doesn't look like
> that."

She, "In dreams I'm your feminine side."

Me, "My feminine side is pretty bad then, huh?"

She, "Yes."

Me, "What's wrong? What should I do? Is it my hair or what?"

She, "It's a matter of vim!" (Where she puts her energies!)

She changed before my eyes and became less straggly and with my hair and a blue dress.

A male counselor had this dream encouraging him to work with the feminine point of view also in mind. The tidal wave may represent the emotional waves which are typically considered female. The dream shows what a beautiful and artistic expression of this balance he is achieving.

Came to swimming pool with a large blackboard beside it. I was to teach a senior lifesaving class (his counseling work) along with a female instructor.

A few little kids came in and started swimming around. A few adults (over 17) came in to sign up for the class. Then the female instructor showed up.

The kids created a tidal wave in the pool and I was watching for kids in trouble.

Female instructor was mad at kids too because they had picked at the new pool paint. Pool was very artistic now—alcoves appeared, one with a lifesize silhouette of a magenta man and woman. Other alcoves with monochromatic prints of pages that

would be the class's yearbook. (His counseling work with male/female balance will
lead to many artistic expressions.)

Another pair of opposites that gives people a lot of
trouble is dominance and submission. It almost seems
like half of the people are wet noodles flopping in whatever direction they are pushed and that the other half
are the pushy ones.

One teacher who was inclined to be a spoiled brat,
but was trying not to, had these dreams one night. It
was as a review of her daily activities because she had
given in and gone where the husband wanted to go that
night instead of insisting on her own way.

1. I dreamed P.G. had died.

P.G. was the worst spoiled brat she had ever had in
any class. Her spoiled brat self had been dealt a death-
blow that day. In the next dream, B.C. is a friend's
husband who is very submissive to his wife.

Dreamed B.C. was suffering a heart attack and we were taking him on a train. I
was nursing him. The train went by a
murky lake and I looked out over the lake
and saw a beautiful sunrise. The train
entered a tunnel; B.C. had a new attack. I
was afraid he might die.

The second dream seems to say, nurse this submissive
quality to health and life. There was a beautiful beginning but watch out for new attacks of resentment, etc.,
or it might die.

Later, this woman had a relapse into being a spoiled brat and she had this dream. L.J. is a friend who has the same problem — she has a snit if she doesn't get her own way. In this dream, L.J. represents the bratty part of the dreamer herself and how she had behaved that day.

> I dreamed L.J. kept insisting that we go to a particular theater. There was no movie on, just a bar on one side of the theater. A man there took L.J.'s arm and pushed her a little. She became violently hysterical. She laid down across two or three seats and was kicking and screaming.
>
> I went to a lobby-kitchen-like place to find a paper towel and wet it for her. The faucets (emotional outlets) were mislabeled and at first I got hot water. Finally I got the towel wet and took it to her. I found they'd gone outside and that her husband had her calmed down. My husband, her husband and I were embarrassed because we were with this hysterical girl.

In other words, the dreamer that day had looked as bad as a grown woman having a tantrum in public just because a man pushed her a little. She had violently over-reacted to her husband's request to do something he wanted to do!

Some people are too serious and forget to enjoy life with a childlike abandon. So, while some people are dreaming that they shouldn't let themselves act like a spoiled child, others are dreaming that they shouldn't suppress the playful childlike self. An overly conscientious schoolteacher, wife and mother dreamed:

> I'm teaching summer school (working during playtime). I have a little girl (her own 'little-girl-self'). Each day I give her a treat—a choice between a chocolate mountain drop or a chocolate honeycomb. She chooses a mountain drop (her 'little-girl-self' wants a mountain of sweet treatment).
>
> I explain to someone I have her rinse her mouth with water afterward (the dreamer tends to feel guilty if she lets herself relax and play a little and, therefore, punishes, washes her mouth out, if she gives herself a treat).

A very domineering man, Adler would say he had a power complex, had this dream. Everyone in the dream study group could see the message except him. All too often this is the case.

> In my mailbox at work I found a box with three plastic pigs' heads in it. Thought, 'those aren't mine, they belong to Mr. J. K. *for making puppets.*' I looked closely; one pig head had pig skin, but bad wolf features and teeth.

This person is pig-headed! Just like the dreamer thinks J.K. is pig-headed and tries to make puppets of other people. It is also a wolfish way to act. Since teeth often symbolize speech, it indicates that he has been using words to intimidate people.

On the other side of the coin are the submissive people. They have a hard time overcoming habits of acting like mice, not men.

> I was in a kitchen. I noticed two mice. They just sat there like they owned the place. I thought, "They must figure they've been around so long and never been bothered that no one cares if they are in the kitchen." They were very fat. Their insolence made me mad and I decided to go after them. I waved at them with my hands, because I couldn't find anything around to really get them. They didn't move. I got a wet red blouse from the wash sink. I wrung it out and swung with it. They moved a little; I got a porcelain pan and came down after them. They jumped on a plate of ham scraps that was on the floor.

When this woman saw her dream as saying that she was habitually too mousey (two mice), it made complete sense to her. The ham scraps had to do with the way she had run like a mouse from a little group attention at a party the night of the dream. It was really acting like a 'ham' and it caused a 'scrap' (fight) with her husband. So, the next time she got with the group she decided not to be too mousey. She managed to make a few remarks in the conversation. That night she dreamed:

> I had two mice which I traded for a kitten.

She realized that in her eagerness not to be mousey she had resorted to making small 'catty' remarks!

The persona is the person as presented to society, our mask of manners we adopt to meet the demands of society. The 'private life' behind the mask may be very different.

Dreams often comment on the outer covering which we showed during that day or which is habitual to us. Since it is our outer covering, its condition is often represented in dreams by our skin or our clothing.

> 1. Dreamer looked in a mirror but instead of his reflection he saw a 'stuffed shirt.'

He had been stuffy that day in relationship to some of his wife's friends.

> 2. Dreamer was driving his car. A friend in the back seat asked, "What kind of work do you do?" As dreamer started to answer the horn began to honk and wouldn't stop. It was stuck.

This dreamer worked at 'tooting his own horn' incessantly!

Those tendencies of our personality which we have not lived, be they good or bad, are called the shadow. As the persona is usually a pleasant mask we present for society, the unlived thoughts we bury behind this are a part of the shadow. In dreams these unknown (subconscious) possibilities are often represented as foreigners of various races or being dark, shadowy parts of our self may be represented as black folks. While unacknowledged, these aspects rob our psyche of energy.

> Dreamer is in a police office and is being interrogated about a crime he was supposed to have committed. He couldn't remember the crime but felt he was being falsely accused.

The dreamer was questioning himself about something unknown. A few nights later he dreamed again but this time he is the police officer as well as being a traveler.

> Dreamer is just entering a motel room with a suitcase of clothes. A robber breaks into the room and tries to steal the suitcase. Dreamer, now a policeman, comes and shoots the robber. Then on a freeway with his girlfriend going home.

The shadowy robber tries to steal his clothes which represent his personality. But he is able to stop the theft. Then he is on the freeway with his girlfriend. This tells us in what area — male/female relationship — his shadow has been acting up. Now he will have a freer way with this area of his life.

Shadow figures are usually of the same sex as the dreamer. This woman is also killing out some of her shadowy aspects.

> Someone was chasing a criminal into our house. The criminal was my daughter all dressed in dark clothing. The authorities went upstairs to get her. I thought she had snuck out a window but we saw her legs, in dark stockings, hanging — she had hung herself. (The dreamer is catching up with a childish "hang up.")

Many people keep the shadowy, selfish tendencies in check with society but then lose control of them in the home. One such woman was guided to look for help from her husband in overcoming this situation.

> Dreamed I was a prostitute. I was being bossy and aggressive in an argument with my cleaning lady. The real me was observing the argument. A voice said, "She (meaning the prostitute) won't live long. What do you think will kill her?"
>
> Real me asked, "Will her husband get her money and their motel business when she dies?"
>
> Voice, "Yes."
>
> Dreamer, "Then I think her husband will do her in."

The dreamer and her husband worked on her being so nice to others and so bitchy at home. As the bossy, prostituted self died out the husband got more of her goodness.

A woman who had a very hard time being patient with her family members, store clerks, etc., etc., had several distressing dreams. She kept dreaming:

> I am in charge of a ward in an institution for the mentally retarded. The retarded patients (patience) are always giving me a lot of trouble.

This could also have meant that she was retarded in her use of her mental abilities because she reacted to situations emotionally instead of thinking about things and seeing the logic behind how other people acted.

Anyway, her mentally retarded patience needed to be brought under control.

The use of one's faculty for good judgment is definitely the theme of this dream.

> Dreamer was at a faculty meeting which had been called to discuss the new school buildings to be constructed.
>
> One faculty member said, "Tell the judges we want concrete buildings."
>
> Dreamer said, "Tell them in a way that sounds half joking and half in deadly earnest."
>
> Principal said, "Why do we need such permanent buildings?"
>
> Dreamer said, "People will need *concrete judgment* buildings forever—even after this school population is gone."

Not only does the dreamer need to use concrete judgment in evaluating a current life experience (lesson, this school population) but will always need to build concrete judgment as a permanent habit(ation).

This principle of self-improvement through dreams was known even in ancient times. The most famous ancient authority on dreams was the Greek Artemidorus. In his writings 18, Vol. IV, Chapter I, he said, "Dreams and visions are infused into man for their advantage and instruction."

What lesson will you be given tonight? Will you be paying attention?

Chapter 7

Quiet, Genius at Work

*It would be no great paradox
to say that the creative work of
genius was excellent dreaming
and that dramatic dreaming was
distracted genius.* *

"Mom, it's so weird! Positively weird!" Allen exclaimed as he burst through the door returning from his high school mid-term exams.

"What's so weird?" asked mom.

"Weird, weird! What happened in the geography test today. Weird!"

Mom is getting worried now. She had insisted he go with her to the hospital and visit grandma last night. Even though he kept saying, "But I haven't studied for my geography test. Not at all, I've been too busy working on that horrible English to study my geography. I

---

*Mandsley, in *Journal of Mental Science,* Jan. 1909, p. 16.

figured I'd do it tonight since I had the English test today."

"What happened, Allen, what was so weird?" mom asked.

"Well," said Allen, "I read the first question, it seemed sort of familiar and I knew, I knew the answer. Second question, same thing happened. Third question, same thing. And then I remembered. Man, is this weird! Mom, honestly, I remembered and the rest of the test proved it. Last night I dreamed that whole test AND ALL OF THE ANSWERS..."

It was the first, last and only, so far, experience of this kind for the fourteen year old boy. But when he needed a problem solved, his dreams came through. Other sleep learning situations have been reported in dream literature. Sometimes sleeping on the book is used as a primer for the dreaming mind.

When sleep closes down the waking mind, with its book knowledge and limited expectancies, often a synthesis takes place and a new idea is born. There are several well known cases where scientific problems have been solved — worked out — by the dreaming mind.

An important chemist who received his most famous insight in a dream is Friedrick Kekule. In 1858 he published his doctrine that the atoms link together to form compounds. This is such common knowledge today it seems obvious but it was a new idea in his day. These linked atoms making compounds were dubbed "Kekule's Sausages." Without the scientific instruments of our day, he was making an intuitive hypothesis but it showed what to look for. In 1865 he published his "brilliant prediction" that the carbon atoms in benzene were linked to form a hexagon. Where did he get such a notion? From a dream of two snakes which came together in a ring by each taking into its mouth the tail of the other. In the dream he 'knew' this represented the forming of the carbon atoms into a 'benzene ring'. Today, chemistry still names the two kinds of organic compounds as 'open chain' or 'ring' derivatives.

His 'startling hypothesis'—demonstrated to him in his dream—paved the way for understanding the chemical structure of the multitude of ring compounds.

In 1936 the Nobel Prize in physiology and medicine went to the German scientist, Otto Loewi. He had been studying the nervous system. One night he dreamed of an experiment with two frogs which showed that the nerves release a chemical when they transmit an impulse. He wrote down the experiment and went back to sleep. Next morning he couldn't read his notes so was unable to try the experiment. That night he dreamed the same dream, wrote notes and again was unable to read them in the morning. The third night when the dream was repeated, he got up, dressed and went to his laboratory. There he took the chemical substance produced in the vagus nerve by the action of one frog's heart. When placed on the heart of another frog, this nerve substance, acetylcholine, stimulated the heart action of the second frog. That was as he said, "An unbelievably simple experiment." Some claim that he later remembered having thought of the experiment while awake eighteen years earlier. Even so, it took his dream mind to remember and insist that it be acted upon.

I'm giving the whole story of these two chemical discoveries so you can see the difference. In one, the information needed, the experiment, was given in a literal fashion. In the other, the carbon atoms were represented or symbolized by the two snakes.

> Singer, the American inventor, tried for many years to develop a mechanism that would accomplish by mechanical means the same thing that a person performs when passing the thread back and forth below and above material; that is, a machine that could stitch. All his attempts seemed to lead into blind alleys. When he was about to give up his search, he dreamed of
>
> > *A long row of knights, armored, dressed in iron mail. Each of them carried a long, sharp lance, resting them on their stirrups. What was interesting was a hole, clearly visible near the sharp end of the lances.*
>
> As Singer woke up he realized that the specific 'trick' needed to accomplish sewing by machine was to place the hole not near the dull end as it is in the hand-sewing needle, but near the sharp end.*

*From the *Twilight Zone of Dreams* by Andre Sonnet as translated by Tony Frazer. Copyright © 1961 by the authors. Reprinted with the permission of the publisher, Chilton Book Company, Radnor, Penn.

I shudder to think how backward civilization would be if Freud had gotten hold of that dream! This points out the importance of interpreting any dream in terms of the dreamer's current life!!

In all of these historic incidences the dreamer had been working on the problem consciously for quite some time—more about that later. Most of us aren't working on such deep, important problems. However, the problem solving aspects of dreaming are available even for the average person's small problems.

Henry had just spent about two hundred dollars to have a new electric sign placed in front of his business. He was pleased and proud when he switched it on the first night and drove home to dinner. The next evening, however, he was not so happy—his sign wouldn't switch on. He looked around for the trouble and was late for dinner. He could hardly wait for business hours the next day to call and tell that electrician off.

That night he dreamed that there was an intermediate switch between the sign and the wall switch he'd been using. First thing in the morning he went to his place of business and checked. Sure enough, behind the post just the way he dreamed it, was another switch. Now he suspected why the son of the businessman next door had giggled and run away yesterday. He must have seen the switch and flipped it off. Well, from now on, thanks to his dream, Henry would be sure to check both switches.

One of our teachers had been given a particularly difficult group of ghetto children as her assignment for the next school year. She was very worried about handling the discipline and motivation of these students. Then she had this dream.

> We had just had a faculty meeting. The school year was ending. There was a shopping cart of supplies for next year by the door. One box, I noticed, was opened and had many little prize toys, badges, a toy airplane, etc. One of the teachers was coming into the room with a group of children. I felt we should put the cart away so we would have all the stuff we needed for next year.

You guessed it. She set up a system of badge recognition, for good behavior and prize earning for work completed. It worked terrifically!

Sometimes the idea is worked out consciously and what we get is a dream prognosis for the outcome.

> I dreamed I was driving along in my car. A radio announcer said my husband's company was looking for a rocket launcher. I thought that was great, they would need someone like me who was agile and had quick reflexes. Then I saw myself in a field launching a rocket affair sort of thing. Then I thought I would also have an advantage since my husband worked there he could help me get the job.
>
> Next, I was in an office interviewing for the job. I explained that I was agile and had quick reflexes. I felt that the interview went well and I would probably get the job.

This dreamer had a project she wanted to launch. The dream seemed to encourage her to go ahead with it and to solicit support from her husband. She soon had a successful launching of her project. It took off like a rocket!

Another woman with an activity, symbolized by the young man, which she was interested in promoting dreamed this prognosis. The trouble seemed to come when the activity tried to involve (take advantage of) a sweet young thing.

> Dreamed of a young man who was secretly making 'white lightning.' The police came to his job and looked around, but found nothing. A young girl worked with the young man and he asked her to carry the stuff in a candy dish down the road. As she was walking down the lonely road, she heard the police car coming and became frightened, but the young man drove up and took the dish from her and drove away. She watched him disappear around a bend and the police followed. When she reached the bend she saw the young man's car had overturned and the police were standing around.
>
> I woke up.

Following this dream, she saw the need to revise her plans.

Art is another area where dreams can activate creativity. The Association of Humanist Artists has an exhibition of artworks based on dream imagery and including the dream text which inspired each artwork. In her book, *The Dream Game,* Dr. Ann Faraday gives a good example of artist creativity from the life of Irene Rice Pereira. There is a complete description of how Ms. Pereira developed new techniques of using light and space in her paintings. Here again, readers may think—well and good for famous people but what about average people.

My sister is the art supervisor for a large school district. Not famous, just an average artist. She contributed two examples of dream help with her art work.

> I am in a school helping teachers. One is doing very little in her classroom. She reels off all of the reasons why. Another has a terrific child-made rendering of her dress pattern. It gives me a great idea which I enthusiastically pass on to the teachers. We will do some pilot programming; comparing classrooms where kids are given specific instruction in seeing and putting down on paper visual concepts such as texture, line, shape, color, in forms that don't cut off creative expression—in fact that lead to creative expression because of increased awareness of visual elements. I see this in my dream as a possible focus for a sabbatical project.

Later, in reality, I wrote a sabbatical proposal to include a component for research at school sites, with children, using creative visual learning games with the focus on the visual elements. I had hesitated asking for the sabbatical because I couldn't think of something worthwhile doing for the district and also interesting to me. This was it!

I submitted the sabbatical request including the research in creativity component—and a couple of nights later I dreamed:

> I am showing some people the teaching materials and packages which I have developed. They are impressed. I am pleased.

Her sabbatical leave was granted!

Another experience my sister had was with a calendar which appeared in her dreams. The colors were vivid and the design elements intriguing. Next day when she was asked to give a presentation at a forthcoming county art teachers workshop, she had a great idea. She created, in reality, the bicentennial calendar of her dream! A great idea for spring 1975, it would be useful for the entire coming year!

An interior decorator reported this experience which became one of the main elements in her approach to individualizing decor. It is an idea uniquely her own.

> I saw some window displays in homes and businesses. Each window display was designed to express the personality, occupation or hobby of the resident, executive or business. I saw two examples in detail. One showed a scope and sequence flow chart in colors on the glass. The other was of a skier. I realized in the dream that the design should use about 20-40% of the window and leave 60-80% for the light to come in. The more the covered area, the

more white was used in the design. Some
seemed to have three dimensional elements.

One dream student who had done a lot of her own
sewing had this experience.

> I saw myself in a red silk, print, floor
> length skirt with a matching sleeveless,
> scoop-neck blouse. The hip length blouse
> was worn outside the skirt. Next, I saw my-
> self wearing the same blouse with matching
> bell bottom pants. This time the blouse was
> tucked in and there was a wide cumber-
> bund around my waist. I observed myself
> turn around like a model and I loved the
> outfit. Then I put on a long sleeved, wide
> collared, full length coat of matching ma-
> terial. Every piece was simple, straight lines,
> the tiny flowers on the red silk were just the
> right touch. It was simply elegant! So
> California!

She became quite frustrated for a while because she
couldn't find any patterns for this design. Finally she
decided she had to have that outfit and besides she had
spotted just the right material. So, since every piece
was very simple, she decided to try doing it without a
pattern. Thanks to the prodding of her dreams she
now knows she can design her own creations without
store bought patterns. She is thrilled!

Amber was another seamstress in one of my dream
classes. A very accomplished designer who made her
living sewing outfits for others. She also designed
'smashing outfits' for herself. Every week we looked

forward to her appearance in something unusual and striking—including self-designed hats! Some of her inspirations also come to her in dreams. Here are a couple of examples in her own words.

"I had always wanted an old-fashioned, very feminine dress but somehow I didn't want the same styles that you see all over. Then one night as I thought about it, I went to sleep and started dreaming:

> I was in a garden, walking, but almost like jumping with every step; I would go high in the air as if I were a feather. I was supposed to be modeling this dress because every time I jumped up, like in slow motion, I would say, "Look!", and in different positions every time, turning all around.

"The dress was white with tucks all over and narrow lace trim; it had a cumberbund with four buttons on the side front, long sleeves, high collar. It was different (or so I thought).

"I made it and that got to be my favorite dress because everytime I wear it, I feel light, happy and beautiful."

Amber's second story involves one morning of waking with an inspirational answer to a problem and a second morning of waking with a strange dream memory.

"I was asked to make a wedding dress for a girl that was pregnant (5 months). She was very cute and petite, but was beginning to 'show.' I had to come up with a design that would 'hide' her condition. I tried several ideas but none of them satisfied me or her.

"One morning, out of the blue, I just woke up with the idea that I instantly drew on paper and got to work on it. I wanted to trim it with dried flowers and make a crown of the same for the headpiece. The fabric was a Georgette sheer, off-white, with a very pale print on pink, yellows, blues and greens, with the lining of silk satin in off-white.

"When I finished it, I was so pleased and so was the girl. That night I had this dream:

> A girl with no face coming to thank me for making her dress over again. She never got to wear it for her own wedding because she died before the day. She was wearing exactly the same dress in my dream and said she told me how to make it. I said, "No!" That it was my own idea, but she kept insisting she 'came over' (from the death side of life) to tell me what she wanted and I just followed instructions. She even said, "When have you ever heard of dried flowers on a dress?" She said they were fresh when she had it.

"For this wedding everybody kept asking me the same question, 'Where did you get the idea for the dress?' They loved it, the bride looked beautiful and it was 'different.' Of course, I didn't say how I got the inspiration."

Music is another form of creativity which appears in dreams. On the Merv Griffin television interview show of August 4, 1974, Steve Allen talked about his song writing. Some songs such as "This Could Be the Start of Something Big" he works out consciously. But he mentioned and then performed one he said came to him in a dream. Its very appropriate title and first line is, "I Had a Dream Last Night About My Old Piano."

Here is a similar example of musical creativity inspired from a dream, but where the music itself was not heard in sleep as is sometimes the case.*

Anton Rubinstein (1829–1894), the Russian composer, had an interesting experience to report. It concerns the fact that his third piano concerto is a musical expression of a dream that he had!

I found myself in a temple where the various instruments of the orchestra seem to have gathered, with the piano contributing his (part) seriously. The orchestra instruments subjected the piano to a difficult examination and they forced him to play different melodies and accords; then they announced in a fiery tone that the piano cannot be considered as being one of them any more. The deep tones of the piano seized upon this occasion and began to cry bitterly. Then the piano collected itself bravely, declaring that it was going to create for itself its own orchestra.

---

*From the *Twilight Zone of Dreams* by Andre Sonnet as translated by Tony Frazer. Copyright © 1961 by the authors. Reprinted with the permission of the publisher, Chilton Book Company, Radnor, Penn.

> *This statement made the other in-*
> *struments so angry that they pushed*
> *the piano out the door.*

Rubinstein translated this dream from a visual experience into an aural experience.

A retired teacher friend of mine, Mabel, also dreams up songs. When I last visited her she played two of her dream songs for me on her organ. They're not at all bad for an amateur and she has had them copyrighted and recorded. In the case of her song, "Tiny Seashells By the Seashore," she dreamed she was on a stage performing and this was the song she sang. With the other one, "My Life Is an Empty Shell," she woke with that phrase and melody in her mind and wrote the rest of the song consciously.

Even I have had creative inspiration in a dream. One night I went and saw a surf movie. There were some beautiful shots of the sunlight sparkling through the waves. I think it was seeing this natural beauty so spectacularly photographed that inspired my subconscious mind. I'm not ordinarily poetic but I woke with this poem complete and set in my mind. Without thought or effort, I recorded it in my dream journal.

> God is in all that we are seeing,
> In Him we move and have our being.
> We have our day and our night,
> But never move from out His sight.
> He is our
> Internal Star.
>
> by Jan Baylis

The Phoenix
Once I wrote a poem in my sleep, a curious Elizabethan lyric . . . called *The Phoenix*. It is not the sort of thing that I have ever written before or since. It came to me the night before my birthday in 1891, I think, when I was staying with a friend at the Dun Bull Hotel, by Hawes Water in Westmorland. I scribbled the lyric down on waking.

> *By feathers green, across Casbeen,*
> *The pilgrims track the Phoenix flown,*
> *By gems he strewed in waste and wood*
> *And jewelled plumes at random thrown.*
>
> *Till wandering far, by moon and star,*
> *They stand beside the fruitful pyre,*
> *Whence breaking bright with sanguine light,*
> *The impulsive bird forgets his sire.*
>
> *Those ashes shine like ruby wine,*
> *Like bag of Tyrian murex split;*
> *The claw, the jowl of the flying fowl*
> *Are with the glorious anguish gilt.*
>
> *So rare the light, so rich the sight,*
> *Those pilgrim men on profit bent,*
> *Drop hands and eyes and merchandise,*
> *And are with gazing most content.*

A.C. Benson 1862–1925
Schoolmaster, don and author.*

Wasn't that a lovely birthday gift and rebirth message from his dream mind!

One night I had a dream which gave me a great idea for an instructional aid in my dream study class.

> I am looking through a book. The pages are divided in half horizontally. The top half told and illustrated the story symbolically as it would appear in any book. The bottom half told and illustrated the story as it would be if translated into its literal or real life meaning.

This works out ideally when applied to the study of fairy tale symbology as related to dream symbology. I've thought of other ways to use this approach but haven't yet executed them.

Another form of creative mental activity in dreams awakens us to new (for the dreamer) thought processes. Here is a good example.

> Joyce T. and I are in my car. We are talking about how a person's house decor reveals their personality. She mentioned that Karen R. (unmarried) had a new unfinished bed and said, "Isn't that a good example?" I agreed. I drove the car up in front of the fancy baroque entrance to Kathy H.'s house. I said, "This is another good example of art and home expressing the personality." I felt I was getting to be a pretty good judge of character by this means.

This was a new way of looking at people as far as this dreamer was concerned. From then on, however, she began to apply this mental process consciously. To quote her, "This is a fascinating and revealing way to study people. Try it!"

Here is another thought expanding dream.

> I'm in a classroom in a small group of students. An instructor is lecturing and uses a lovely large Tiffany lamp to demonstrate his point. His lesson was that the fourth dimension of an object is its effect on people. So that the lamp has the dimension of beauty in its design and color but turn it on and you light up the person's world—that is an added dimension. Apply this to humans, he said, and you discover that the fourth dimension is love from one another and its effect on people's lives. Turn on your love and you will light up the world.

Now I call that good thinking!

A less direct approach, but one I personally approve of, happened to Janie who came to my September 1974 dream study class. Her dream is dated in June 1974.

> I am talking to a pleasant looking woman. She is not anyone I know. We are on the Fullerton State College campus. I ask her about where to take a good class. She shows me a black and white catalog. The cover says: Dreams—Sept. One.

The next day, while at Fullerton State College, Janie casually picked up a North Orange County Community College, Adult Education Division catalog. In it she found listed my dream interpretation class scheduled to start in September!

The Senoi tribe of Malaysia was studied extensively by psychologist Kilton Stewart because of that society's high regard for dreams. There are several points in their approach to dreams and one deals with the creative powers of the dream mind. I took a class from Kilton Stewart's widow, Clara Stewart Flagg, and we discussed the Senoi use of dream creativity. They teach their young children not to fear falling, climbing, traveling or flying dreams. Everyone in their society is trained to use these dreams to arrive at places in the dream universe where the dream characters show them new designs, dances, music or some idea that will be useful to the tribe! In comparing our culture to theirs, Kilton Stewart wrote, "This social neglect of the sleep side of man's reflective thinking, when the creative process is most free, seems poor education."

There are ways that you can increase the creativity of your dreams. First of all, increase the creativity and exposure of your waking life. Expose yourself to beauty in all forms — painting, music, good movies, poetry, literature and nature! Exercise your imagination in day dreams and fantasies. Develop your power of observation, practice noticing and remembering details. As psychology professor Joseph Adelson says, "The ability to stand apart from reality is a necessary first condition for transforming it imaginatively."

Besides these generalized things, there are some things to do when you particularly want a dream to help you with a specific problem. In other words—how to incubate a dream solution.

First of all, be sure you have gathered all the information you can find in the waking world. This provides fragmented information which the dream may synthesize. Just before retiring, review this information in note or outline form. Maybe it will be your feelings on an emotional decision which you have listed in two columns, pro and con.

Then, before falling asleep, suggest to your inner self that you desire help with this particular problem. Pray if need be! Don't give up if you don't succeed the first night, keep trying. And don't be overly emotional or active before trying to get a dream solution. Don't use alcohol or other stimulants or depressives. Try to arrange waking naturally rather than to an alarm; most answering dreams come just before your natural waking time.

I always advise my dream students not to use the approach too frequently because it may block off another message of importance that your dream mind would like to send you. For people especially interested in creative dreaming, there is an excellent book out on that topic. It is *Creative Dreaming* by Patricia Garfield, Simon and Schuster.

Here are some other historical examples of creativity in dreams. The dream mind synthesized elements from that which had occupied the waking mind.

Inventing the Euphonium
On the 2nd of June 1789, being tired with walking, he sat down on a chair, about nine

in the evening, to enjoy a short slumber; but scarcely had he closed his eyes, when the image of an instrument such as he wished for seemed to present itself before him, and terrified him so much that he awoke as if he had been struck with an electric shock. He immediately started up in a kind of enthusiasm; and made a series of experiments which convinced him that what he had seen was perfectly right, that he now had it in his power to carry it in to execution. He made his experiments, and constructed his first instrument in so private a manner, that no person knew anything of it. To this instrument he gave the name Euphon, which signifies an instrument which has a pleasant sound.

— Dr. Ernst Chladni (1756–1827)
German physicist.*

The discovery of the cause and remedy of diabetes by F.G. Banting (1891–1941) the immortal Canadian physician, is also associated with a dream experience. As he relates it, one evening, after a day's futile and tiresome research work spent in attempts to identify the cause of diabetes, he went to bed. In

*From *Gates of Horn and Ivory: An Anthology of Dreams*, compiled by Brian Hill (Taplinger Publishing Company 1968). Copyright © 1967 by Brian Hill. Reprinted by permission.

the middle of the night he woke from his sleep with a jolt; turned on his light, grabbed his notebook, and wrote down three sentences, which were to save the life of thousands since that event.

> *Tie up the duct of the pancreas of a dog. Wait for a few weeks until the glands shrivel up. Then cut it out, wash out and filter the precipitation.* *

Surgical Advice
Galen's three dreams — The third more worthy of being called a miracle, was, when being twice admonished in his sleep, to cut the artery that lies between the fore finger and the thumb, and doing it accordingly, he was afreed from a continual daily pain with which he was afflicted in that part, where the liver is joined to the midriff; and this he has testified at the end of his book of Venesection. 'Tis certainly a very great example, when a man so great as he was in the medicinal art, put so much confidence in a dream as to try experiments on himself; where he was to run the

---

*From the *Twilight Zone of Dreams* by Andre Sonnet as translated by Tony Frazer. Copyright © 1961 by the authors. Reprinted with the permission of the publisher, Chilton Book Company, Radnor, Penn.

risque of his life, in his very own art. I cannot help but admire his probity in the next place, that where he might have arrogated the merit of the invention to himself, and placed it wholly to the account of the subtily, and penetration of his own genius, he attributed it to God, to whom it was due.

Claudius Galenus b. circa 130 A.D.
Greek physician*

*From *Gates of Horn and Ivory: An Anthology of Dreams,* compiled by Brian Hill (Taplinger Publishing Company 1968). Copyright © 1967 by Brian Hill. Reprinted by permission.

Chapter 8

Golden Butterflies

*In the fullness of time all
matter will become the unspotted
mirror of God in which the image
of His goodness will be clearly
reflected.*
—from *The Gnostic Mass*

There is ample evidence that religion and philosophy are a natural, high level aspect of life. Therefore, I make no excuse to people who, because they haven't reached that stage of development, say that religion is a crutch for the weak. A little investigation shows that life on earth is like a preparatory school. As individuals upgrade their life, higher consciousness is achievable. The fundamentalist, organized religions in America are giving way to all kinds of new spiritual growth as these true dreams of present day Americans show. There are no limits in the dream realm, only what the waking consciousness is open to accept. Therefore, the following interpretations are given just as they proved meaningful to the individuals who experienced them.

One of my own to begin with. There is no dream story to tell but I dreamed I heard a band of angels singing the Hallelujah Chorus. It was absolutely magnificent, like no earthly sounds could possibly be. That was it, just a few bars of "the music of the spheres!" Just one experience like that would convince the greatest skeptic that there is more to this life, than this life. Mind you, I had done nothing peculiar to induce this— no drugs, breathing, fasting, etc. It just came to me at a time when I needed encouragement.

Jungian psychologists call the process individuation, others talk about becoming integrated, beyond that we have mystical enlightenment of cosmic-consciousness. Along this path toward union with the universal life forces are many stages and some dangerous side tracks. But I'll let the dreams speak for themselves.

To begin with, what do dreams say about staying with a materialistic approach to life?

'Mrs. Tryer' was a member of a spiritual study group. Her next door neighbor bought some new dining room furniture, lovely and expensive. 'Mrs. Tryer' had adequate dining furniture, but nonetheless, she pestered her husband to buy a new expensive set. In fact, it was hard for her not to fall into a pattern of trying to 'keep up with the Joneses.' Her dream:

> 'Mrs. Crude', a friend, was making me a new black and white dress. I said, "Let me know the cost of the material and I'll pay you. Also, I owe you for the material in the

> black and white dress you made me before.
> I'll also pay you for the patterns."
>
> I had a strong feeling of guilt and really
> wanted to get paid up.

She associated to the symbols in this way:

'Mrs. Crude'—a material-minded person, lesser self.

new dress—attitude shown, worn, that day.

I'll pay—law of cause and effect, karma.

I owe—being in debt or behind in payments.

black and white—conflicts or too extreme, trouble between self and husband.

patterns—form being followed, habitual behavior.

guilt feeling—urging to improve.

"The dream not only points out my bad attitude, but seems to warn me that if it is indulged in much more it could become a karmic problem," said 'Mrs. Tryer'.

A man who was beginning to be interested in bridging the gap between himself and God was told by his teachers that a life of service to others was part of the deal. His dreams made comment.

> A doctor was helping some men build a
> bridge in South America. Though I was
> only watching, I felt identity with the
> doctor. He was holding up a part and the
> other men began to seal him in with the
> concrete material up to his neck (he was
> imbedded in the material).
>
> A golden angel came and demanded his
> release. It was the guardian angel of a man
> dying in a hospital. He needed this doctor.

> A blue angel, guardian angel of the doctor, also came.
>
> The workmen tore away the concrete and freed the doctor to go and save the dying man.

He saw the doctor as healing influences and the need to be of service to others. They were building a bridge or way to cross over from material world to contact spiritual influences. He felt a message that he had been too concerned with material existence, but that service to others was the way to his salvation and release.

Another man who had become quite interested in the higher life had these dreams:

> I am in a restaurant with 'Mr. Seeker', another member of my church group. We give the cashier a dollar. For change he gives me four quarters and an extra gold quarter. I give the gold quarter to my friend.

The dictionary definition of a quarterback is: "the player whose position is behind the line of scrimmage, and who generally calls the signals." God is behind our life which is on the line of scrimmage! If we let Spirit call the signals, we receive an extra quarter. The quarterbacking he receives in exchange for what he puts into his church affiliation (his spiritual efforts as well as tithes) come back to him increased and with greater value (gold).

When they went to 'cash in' (he said this might mean after death), they received better than whole! He also saw a relationship to casting your bread upon the water.

Another dream he had pointed out that the spiritual (symbolized by the temple) is better than the best of the material (symbolized by the gold).

> I am talking to an East Indian, he says, "There is something finer than gold. It says so in the scriptures in Matthew."

The dreamer looked and found in Matthew 23: 16–17, Jesus said, "Whether is greater, the gold or the temple that sanctifieth the gold?"

Often new spiritual growth requires that one give up previous ideas which may have been carefully instilled in one's childhood. At this point a dream on this topic will most likely appear. For example, a young woman named April had read and thought about *The Aquarian Gospel of Jesus the Christ* by Levi. Then she dreamed:

> I went into the old family church wearing a dress with levi pants under it and high-heeled shoes.
>
> Most of the congregation were Indian and Mexican. I sat down beside my mother (who is deceased). I felt weird and left. My mother left with me.

In associating with the symbols in the dream, April said her dress was inappropriate for church, or unorthodox; Indians and Mexicans she thought of as deprived and repressed; for her this mother church was deceased. The high-heeled shoes seem to say she wants higher understanding. Put it all together and it tells her — attending this church makes you feel deprived and repressed. You feel weird because what you want is unorthodox. Even so, in an unorthodox church you may find that higher understanding you seek.

Cathy had been raised a Catholic but was now strongly attracted to a metaphysical church. She had this interesting dream:

> My dead brother and I are in a long hall (her change in religious belief has been a long haul). We are taking down Christmas (Christ-mass) decorations. My dead brother is rolling up the tinsel (tinsel and trapping of the old religion are now dead for her).
>
> There is a large blue ornament near the top of the tree. He says, "No, don't take that one down without a ladder." (Some of the meanings of the past religion are high on the ladder of spiritual learning—keep them in sight).
>
> They go out to a beautiful huge green lawn (expansive growth). The lawn is covered with sparkling water (spiritual nourishment). We walk through the water and come to a large house—our home (her expanding consciousness). There is a warm fire in the fireplace (spiritual fires and warmth of spirit). A dream phone rang and I woke up (she's getting the message).

Another of Cathy's dreams which advises an overthrow of her religious background.

> I'm moving from my apartment (feeling of separation from God) into a home with a huge living room (expanded consciousness of life). There are three doors on one wall. I choose the middle door (a middle

> way—not too extreme). Through the middle door I come to a huge backyard which needs some fixing. One thing I plan to clear out of the yard is a shed. Inside the shed I find a Catholic nun teaching children.

Later in Cathy's metaphysical studies, she began to get glimpses into higher levels of consciousness and life beyond physical death. Cathy felt this next dream was both a progress report and a promise.

> I'm with my sister who died last May. We are moving into a split-level house (levels of consciousness including the higher plane where her sister continues to live). My sister shows me my bedroom. The carpet on my floor is gold (valuable understanding). There are four small windows with white curtains (the outlook is pure though she can't see through this level except in spots). My sister's floor is bare so I give her some scatter rugs (understanding on that level is lacking but scattered pieces of understanding are coming).

Sometimes it is hard for us to realize that our religion is not the only right one. But all religions have some truth and the universal truths are true whatever religion expounds them. Here is an example from the Edgar Cayce readings.

Question 1. Sunday morning, August 23, 1925, at home in Deal.
Dreamed I had an earache and was waiting for my mother in front of Katz and Bestoff's,

a drug store in my old home, New Orleans.
My mother came and my ear hurt so, I
wanted her to take me to a doctor. "You don't
need one," she said. "You can overcome that
yourself." I did and it so surprised me that I
went driving with my friend C.C. and told
her all about it. "What you need," she said,
"is Christian Science. You ought to try it, for
that is Christian Science. Become a Christian
Scientist." "No," I replied, "I have my own
Science—Jewish Science. I cured myself, just
naturally."
Answer 1. In this we see the presentation of
the truths as are manifest in the physical
world that are loathe to be gathered in a
physical experience; for as is seen, the forces
which are manifest to bring the relief to
physical force are not of a one faith, but a
oneness in faith in the God-force manifest in
the individual, see? Study then those truths,
for they remain a oneness, whether Jewish,
Gentile, Greek, or heathen.

Edgar Cayce Reading 136-12

The man who had the next dream was not even
interested in religion, consciously that is. But his psyche
was ready to move in that direction. He got involved
in dream recording through counseling because of
employment problems. He dutifully recorded this
dream around Christmastime 1972.

I was suddenly involved in taking a trip
to Israel. I was checking my luggage and

> discovered I had left without my shoes, my
> camera and my medicine. I was told meals
> would be served twice daily at 10 and 2. I
> was with two friends doing a hora dance.
> I went out to get the needed shoes, camera
> and medicine.

In August 1973, eight months later, much to his surprise, he went on a group tour (hora is a group folk dance) to Israel. The tour was conducted by Diane Pike, Bishop Pike's widow, and her co-worker, Arleen Lorrance. He wasn't interested in these spiritual aspects of the trip. But subconsciously he was ready. After returning, he laughingly said, "I got a lot out of that trip I hadn't planned on. I found understanding (shoes); got a spiritual healing (medicine); and got the picture (camera) of what the Holy Land symbolizes!" Part of each day was planned to tend to (10–2) the spiritual side of life. Meals in dream, spiritual food for him to tend to. Skeptics beware!

While searching for new spiritual teaching, our dreams keep us posted on our innermost reactions. The reason for the diversity in faiths is that different people need different approaches. When asking, "Is this right for me?", why not check with your dream mind?

Early in my interest in the Edgar Cayce work I was concerned about how it might conflict with my previous religion.

> I had a dream about being at a lecture
> with a girlfriend from my church. A girl
> from ARE study group came and sat on
> my other side. When the lecture was over,
> I introduced them to each other. Then I

> said, "What shall we do about lunch?" The
> friend from church said, "Why don't we go
> together. After all, we're a pair of bare
> peers."

Another new ARE study group member was encouraged by this dream.

> I was in the midst of the hassle of selling
> my house and was looking for a new
> home. I was looking for, and went to, my
> aunt's house. The address was 17 Newport
> Avenue (a real address memory from her
> childhood). I went in the side door.

In numerology, most number interpretation depends on adding the numbers across. This often helps in dreams also. The number 17 added across equals eight. Eight turned on its side (she went in the side door) is a symbol for infinity; never endingness. She is looking for a new port. Her old religion no longer satisfied her needs. Her search ended at a new port with the infinite. She came to feel very at home with the Cayce philosophy.

After starting a spiritual studies correspondence course, Julie reported this dream.

> Dreamed I received a giant vitamin pill
> in the mail. A boss and I were typing up
> some good reports and making carbon
> copies. My reader's guide membership
> needed to be taken care of right away.

The studies, which are good like vitamins, should be shared. Go on to disseminate the information to guide others.

In this instance, the dreamer was shown the harmony that can exist between psychology and religion so that one enhances the other. She had been to a lecture the evening previous to the dream where the lecturer mentioned dreams, etc., as 'flashes of light from the unconscious.' He then showed books to the class which were Gnostic Scriptures. Her dream:

> A large flashlight was shining on a book, "The Gnostic Gospels." A smaller one shone on a Jung text.

Thus, for this student the Gnostic Scriptures will really light up her unconscious spiritual awareness in conjunction with Jungian psychology. She pursued these studies together to great benefit.

Dorothy was newly interested in occult studies, reincarnation and higher states of consciousness. She was getting a lot of 'static' about it from her mother and particularly from the influence she had had on Dorothy when she was just a 'little shaver.'

> I approach a several-storied house (many levels of consciousness). In the living room I'm shaving my legs (smoothing out her support system, getting rid of the fuzziness). I'm using my mother's pink shaver and it is very noisy. I'm checking a hearing mold (for a hard-of-hearing aid).
> I throw it out (she is no longer hard-of-hearing). There is a noise above in the next level of the house (movement on a higher level of her consciousness). I become frightened and run outside (if you've ever felt the

> stirrings of higher consciousness you know it can seem frightening). As I back out the car, I realize I have to be careful not to run down Mr. Newman.

It seems that if she backs out of this experience she may endanger the life of the 'new man.' She is trying to develop the new consciousness within, a new birth within herself. This dream gave her courage to continue and not back away from or run out on her 'new man.' Dorothy was taking a safe meditative approach to the occult.

Pauline got a different message about her occult investigations with a group which used ouija boards, automatic writing and contact with spirit entities. Mr. Ubancheck was a high school teacher in the area. Of all the high school teachers, she knew he was chosen for this dream because of his name. Her dream mind seemed to her to be saying about her investigations, You ban! Check?

> Mr. Ubancheck and I were hugging and kissing and I was liking it! I knew he'd murdered two wives though and that frightened me. When I came up for air and glanced out the window, I saw detectives prowling around investigating and knew they knew, too. Mr. Ubancheck saw them but that didn't stop him. He just smiled and kissed me some more. I was glad I wasn't guilty along with him, but it was an uneasy feeling I had.

The psychic-development class was interesting and attractive, but Dorothy had heard that some avenues of investigation into the unconscious realms are not safe. This could be murderous if she continued!

Another man, attracted to Buddhism, had this dream:

> Dreamed last night of a battle. A phalanx of Oriental persons was in the center, protected by a shield covering. In the end, when the shields were dropped, no one was there.

He was able to interpret this for himself as: Buddhism holds nothing for me, it is as an empty shell.

Our dream mind is there encouraging us to expand. Helen worked for a newspaper. Here is her dream just as she recorded and responded to it.

> I am a reporter covering this story[1] in a large, multi-storied house;[2] all beautiful wood;[3] about a paraplegic[4] whose house it was. I am telling the editor[5] about it, and it is accepted for the paper, then rejected because the editor found out it was a phony story.[6]

Interpretation:

(1) It is my story.
(2) Large, expansive consciousness.
(3) Wouldn't (woodn't) I have a beautiful, large expansive consciousness.
(4) Crippled owner of the consciousness.

(5) Editor (higher self).

(6) Editor not accept phony story, I am not crippled.

She felt the dream said, "Reject your feeling of help-lessness. It's phony. Be your natural (wood) self and the beauties of expanded consciousness can be yours." This dream came two nights in a row as if to emphasize the point it was trying to make.

Any spiritual discipline worth its salt is just that—a discipline. It is easy enough to study some high-minded idealistic philosophy, but is that enough? All the great religious leaders have taught that it doesn't mean much until you apply it. That is where most people, even sincere ones, have trouble. This is the message of these next few dreams had by various people who related them to their spiritual studies and aspirations.

> Hazel:
> 1. Laid out a big spread for Explorer Scouts. My husband was angry because they came and loaded up plates, salad, cheese, cold meat, fruit. He said they came and loaded up their plates but never did anything.
> 2. Some people seemed to think I was a witch. A luminous bird (mine) was flying—it plunged to the earth dead—somehow connected with the death of my father.
> George:
> I had a small plastic bag of peanuts (small growth). Ate a few. Rolled up the bag and rubber banded it closed. Put it in a skin pouch on the side of my foot.

Plastic—not real, no real growth—it's just 'peanuts.'
I know it and it gets under my skin.

> Sue:
> I'm in a restaurant (receiving spiritual
> food) with Dean (her oldest brother who
> she interpreted as an Elder Brother). The
> table is too high for me to reach the food
> if I try to sit at the table. But I come up to
> where the food is if I stand *on my own two
> feet*.

Remember the Biblical parable of the talents? See
Matthew 25:14-30. It has been said that spiritual
knowledge not used is sin. Here's an example of how a
dream can say it:

> I'm walking down a hall and looking
> forward to rearranging my books. My new
> bookcases were two layers deep. The back
> layer for elementary school books was full.
> I have a whole wall of cases for Oriental
> books.
> An Oriental sage in robe and hat is ele-
> vated behind my overstuffed easy chair
> reading an Oriental Bible and saying,
> "Orientals believe a man cannot be born
> a spiritual leader. One can't become a
> spiritual emperor until he begins to work
> as one. He must take a little bit of bread
> (life) and butter (love) and eat it (use it).
> Then he becomes an emperor in the sense
> of a spiritual leader."
> The sage opened a map showing the
> Western World. He said, "That was a pas-
> sive allegory, while some might make an

active allegory and use the symbol of a (great big action and shakeup)." The Los Angeles earthquake of February 1972 woke me up with a jolt.

The earthquake rolled her out of bed! She felt the message was: Time is passing (going down a hallway). Books and studying aren't enough. Elevate yourself above the easy life of reading (chair I usually sit in to read). Get up and apply your philosophy in a really big way! The delicate timing necessary to have that dream arrive at the point of action, just as the earthquake struck, really fascinates me. But the scope in time and space of the dreaming mind is a phenomenon to behold!

Jay was involved in a church group effort. He sincerely did his part very conscientiously. Some group members made very little effort but took more than a fair share of the credit. Jay was feeling resentful and judgmental. Then he had this dream which made him feel much better. It restored his ability to put in the effort he wanted to.

I saw several transparent disks about six inches in diameter. Half of each disk was dark, the other half of each disk was light. The disks were placed on different levels of a stand such as I had seen used for a three dimensional chess game. Looking at the disks, I knew (lucky Jay is getting the dream's interpretation right in the dream, as sometimes happens). I knew each disk represented the effort put into the project by the various group members. The individuals were on different levels but in each case the amount of material effort (represented by the dark half of the disk) was exactly equal to the amount of spiritual gain (represented by the light half of the disk). I knew all of this in the dream.

Much of the new spiritual awakening in the world today hinges on meditation. Not just for Oriental yogas and Christian monks, but as a connecting link between heaven and earth for anyone willing to make the effort.

John wanted to make that effort but after starting he got sidetracked in the press of daily living. One morning he woke with a strange word on his mind and wrote it in his dream journal. Ziggurat. He was quite amazed to find that word two weeks later while skimming through a book by Manly Hall. The book stated, "A Ziggurat is a Chaldean astronomical observation tower —symbolic of a link between heaven and earth." His reaction was that his dreams were reminding him about meditation, that available link between man on earth and God or his own higher self. He returned to his program of daily meditation. This interpretation meets the criterion set forth by Dr. Ann Faraday in her book *The Dream Game*. "A dream is correctly interpreted when it makes sense to the dreamer, when it checks out with his other dreams, and when it moves him forward in his life."—Introduction, p. xiv

One night Jay had this series of dreams about his progress in meditation.

I was riding with R— in his car (R— is a good example of someone who meditates regularly and is a fine man). A group of Oriental men pulled their car in front of us so we had to stop (Oriental sages have taught meditation for centuries). (To meditate, one must stop and be still.) They took us with them to a building and left us just waiting (meditating). They rolled out a man on a cot. He was wrapped in white cloth (white is a spiritual symbol because it is the synthesis of all colors). There was a purple band around him. It was R's turn—he went in willingly—I decided to run away and mingle with the crowd. Outside there were relatives, one offered me some cookies (the distractions of physical goodies).

I woke, recorded that dream and went back to sleep.

I'm on an island (in solitude as in meditation). I was supposed to take care of this island. It was almost covered in water, only a small green area remained above water for me to sit on (I would be forced to sit still). My deceased sister came (a messenger from a higher level). I asked her, "Why so much water?" She said, "The tide is rising" (the rising kundalini forces). I knew I was to be immersed in the waters (baptized into a spiritual life).

I woke, recorded and slept again.

I was back in the building with the Oriental man waiting for the elevator (way to higher consciousness). My boss came up and the Oriental man said he should come with us. I heard a jingle in my throat (occult symbol for will). I pulled a prayer bead out of my throat and started to pray (pray for the will to be reborn). The Oriental man spoke but I felt like it was an inward voice. He said, "You will have to go through with this and while doing it, you might loose your life because you are now breathing the life of the flesh."

I was nearing my forty-first birthday when I began to get interested in meditation. After reading some about it, my consciousness was open to the idea. I had some messages from my dreams urging me to get involved with this process. My dreams promised me great rewards.

I was observing a grandmother and her four year old granddaughter at court. I was conscious that I was both of these dream characters (so far the dream says—how grand you are—observe and judge). The little girl's parents had been killed in an auto accident. The judge gave her into the custody of the grandmother until she became 16 years old (four is considered to be the number of wholeness. In the number 4 the / line symbolizes subconsciousness; the — line symbolizes self-consciousness; the | line symbolizes superconsciousness; 16 is four-squared! Wholeness raised to a higher power! When she reached age 16, the court would make another decision.)

> She had inherited 41 million dollars (I
> was just 41 years old), but the inheritance
> was mostly in desert property and wouldn't
> acquire that value until she was 16. (In the
> Bible, where does Jesus go to commune
> with his Heavenly Father, meditate that is?
> He goes into the desert, an ancient symbol
> for the solitude of meditation.)
> At the end of the dream, the grand-
> mother and the granddaughter drove off
> into the desert to pass the twelve years
> waiting (meditating).

Soon after that, after I had begun meditating, I had
this simple but beautiful dream.

> Two gold rings, one from each side,
> floated into view. They aligned themselves
> in the center of my field of vision and
> formed a wedding set. A voice said, "Medi-
> tate and join the circle of inner-knowing!"

They say that only two things are inevitable — death
and taxes. I'm not about to get into any discussion
about taxes at this point in our history! So, let's talk
about death. Death of the physical body certainly
seems to be inevitable.

How does that affect our dreams? As stated in the
beginning chapter, death is not usually pictured in
dreams as death. Conversely, death in dreams is usually
not a picture of physical death. Here is an example to
illustrate a dream of death that did not mean the literal
death of the person.

Many groups call all females sister and all males
brother because we are all part of the human family.

In this dream, the relationship of sister-in-law was chosen by the dream mind to illustrate the closeness of the friendship involved. The dead woman in the dream was a close friend, not a literal sister-in-law. 'Mr. Advisor' had this dream about 'Mrs. Flounderer:'

> 'Mrs. Flounderer' was my sister-in-law and she had died. It was necessary for me to go to the mortuary for the autopsy. I was embarrassed when I saw her laid out nude, but I knew I had to help with the investigation into her death.

What was really happening? 'Mrs. Flounderer' was attempting to launch a career. 'Mr. Advisor' was a friend who knew quite a lot about what it would take to be successful in this area. He knew she was floundering in her attempt. But she had not asked for his advice. He felt the dream meant she should take a thorough look (autopsy) at the cause of the death of phase one. He felt he could and should help her look at and evaluate the situation even though it might be embarrassing.

Prompted by the dream, he called her and they talked about the dream and the floundering career. She appreciated his help.

Dreams often predict the coming of a literal death, since death is a natural but emotional aspect of life. I personally doubt if it ever comes without a dream notification, but most dreams are not recalled or understood. Here are a couple of examples where people dreamed of their own coming death.

> While driving on the freeway, cars started piling up. I got out of my car (out of her physical body) and walked up ahead to see what the delay was. When I got back to my car it had been crashed into! I realized the insurance company would have to total it out (her body would be totally 'out of it'). I wasn't upset over that but I was upset because my car's lifetime battery was not going to be any good anymore!

This woman died of a heart attack about six months later.

This man dreamed symbolically of his death about a month before it came. His wife correctly interpreted the dream to herself when he had it. There was nothing she could do except make his last month as meaningful as possible. He had made arrangements to go to a special clinic in Arizona. His dream:

> I was in Arizona and went to an air research center (air can mean heaven). I had a new job (new way of making a living, life beyond death). I had to put on all white clothing (white being the color of spirit). In order to go to work in the clean room (heaven), I had to be sterilized (two meanings, to be made impotent and to be purified). My older brother (family representative) was there. I noticed his right hand had one finger cut off (one member will be cut off from the family).

In this next instance, this woman didn't die, but she almost did. She had this dream prior to the onset of the near fatal illness.

I'm back in Ireland where I grew up, walking along a road. A black taxi pulls up beside me. In the taxi are my two brothers and my father (all of whom are deceased). We are about a mile from the graveyard. One of my brothers gets out of the taxi and says, "Get in, we'll give you a ride." My foot is on the edge of the taxi when my father speaks, "No! Get out now!"

I back away and the taxi drives on. I turn the other way and now I am walking with my brother-in-law (who had recently survived a heart attack). He said, "Don't look back." But I did look and the black taxi was gone.

Frequently dream premonitions of the death of a loved one come in symbolic form. Some people seem to be more tuned to this than others. One friend has a recurring death symbol. Whenever she dreams of two rings she knows it means a coming death. Two large rings signify the death of a close friend or near relative, medium sized rings foretell the death of distant relatives and small rings signify acquaintances.

Judy foresaw the death of her uncle in this dream.

I saw my uncle on a stretcher in the kitchen of our home. Everyone was standing around very anxious about him. He got up off the stretcher, walked outside, got into a black car and drove into the woods. Then he parked the car, got out and walked to the banks of a river. He proceeded to collect sticks of wood and make a raft. He stepped onto the raft, tipped his hat to us, and drifted out of sight.

The stretcher indicated illness. Black is the color of the unknown; the car is the vehicle or body which houses the soul. Woods often represent unknown territory or the unconscious and the river, the river of life. From the foregoing, it was evident the gentleman was about to die or as the ancients would say, "Cross the river Styx" (sticks). We asked the dreamer if her uncle was ill. She said, "No." This was on a Monday evening. Wednesday morning she received an urgent call from home. Her uncle was dead.

Even though Carrie did not get along well with her brother, Lyle, and they were separated by thousands of miles, her dreams foretold his death.

> Someone was taking me through a tenement house. The rooms were small and poor (we are temporary tenants of the earthly plane our bodies are small and difficult for the spirit to abide in). We stopped in one room where I saw what had been my mother's piano. It was dilapidated and made no sounds. I thought, of course, it would be like that, she has been dead for many years. In the room also was a table with a picture on it. I recognized it as a family picture I had come across last summer while cleaning out a closet. It seemed strange. Then I realized that one boy was turned around and I was seeing the back of his head! The guide said, "That is Lyle." Then the back of the room seemed to open up and I heard music and saw a beautiful sunset. Then the guide took me back out of the tenement building.

The tenement building could have represented the family life of her childhood because she said it was a poor and unharmonious family. But she clearly felt that her brother was coming to the sunset of his life. She received word that morning that Lyle had passed on. ·

In spiritual studies, the topics of death and life after death naturally come up for instruction and discussion. After such a lesson, one woman had this dream:

> I dreamed I died and was being taken into the Presence. There was no Great Being that I could see, but I knew I was in the Presence and a voice said, "Give an accounting of your life."
>
> I said, "There is no accounting for it. I just lived it." The voice said, "Very good— that's right—you lived it."
>
> I felt accepted into the realm of the Presence.

This lovely bit of insight seemed to be triggered by a lecture the dreamer had been to that evening on the subject of death. The speaker had said that if you die and see a light and follow it you are sure to be all right.

> I'm in an old frame house with windows to the floor. On the third or fourth floor with K.H., a friend who had recently been at death's door. There was an earthquake and we fell out of the house. I started to say The Lord's Prayer. Stopped and worried a minute, then started The Lord's Prayer again. What better thing could I do while dying? Woke up.

That one was followed by this one, the same night:

> Saw a point of light. It came toward me.
> I was shot through with a tingling feeling
> and said, "Thank you, God. Oh, thank
> you." I felt wonderful!

As the religions of the East and the West become more combined we find many Americans accepting the premise of reincarnation. Benjamin Franklin, as well as many other famous personalities, have believed in rebirth both literal and symbolic. He wrote his own epitaph when he was twenty-two years old.*

> "The body of B. Franklin,
> Printer,
> Like the cover of an old book,
> Its contents torn out
> And
> Stripped of its lettering and gilding,
> Lies here
> Food for worms,
> But the work shall not be lost,
> For it will as he believed
> Appear once more
> In a new and more elegant edition
> Revised and corrected
> By the author."

The following dreams were interpreted *by the dreamers* to be glimpses of past lives. These dreams

*From *Reincarnation—An East-West Anthology* by Head & Cranston.

were meaningful to them according to that interpretation which meets my criteria for a good interpretation. Notice the Alice in Wonderland, down the rabbit hole, type of entrance to some of these dreams.

> It is evening and I'm walking down a sidewalk in a *tract of houses* (series of lives). I come to some bushes which are blocking the sidewalk. I push them out of my way and find myself in bright sunshine in a beautiful country. I am amazed! Next thing I know I'm in some type of old house or cabin. There is a young peasant couple there and I feel a strong identity with the young woman. He says, "Why are you eating that meat?" He speaks with a strong Irish accent. She answers that her church is a long way away and they won't know. I then begin trying to find my way out of there. It is old and rather dark. Finally I pry open a window. A voice asks me why I'm leaving and why I'm crying. Then I realize that I am crying and that I'm leaving a place that means something to me — but I do leave.

The dreamer was embracing reincarnation and many new religious ideas and was consciously convinced of their truth. She felt this dream meant that she had once lived as an Irish Catholic as well as being born an American Catholic in this life. That, she said, would explain why she felt so sad about leaving the Catholic faith when she really believed in the truth of her new religion. The experience was meaningful to her!

Another young woman had this dream experience which she felt was a glimpse of a past life.

> I'm watching a circus performance. A tiger gets loose and the crowd is filled with fear. I begin to run through the stands or a hole. Suddenly there is an old fashioned horsedrawn carriage. All in black and the passengers are dressed in black. I watch the carriage drive through an old fashioned New England town square. Then it curves off to the right and I rest my eyes on a tombstone. Next, an old elephant comes through the town square followed by a couple of colorful carriages and a woman in a red dress. I feel very sad for her and the hard traveling life I know she lives. I wake up feeling glad that it is now.

In trying to find meaning in this dream, the emotional feeling seems to be the biggest help. Fran said the main thing was how sorry she felt for the woman in the red dress and how glad she was to wake up and find herself in her present life. Her thought was that she had been a traveling circus performer in a life in the last century and that it had been a hard life.

The amount of spiritual guidance in this next dream is fantastic. The dreamer is a woman who had joined an A.R.E. "Search for God Study Group." This led to a questioning interest in reincarnation. Her dream is long but very worthwhile to demonstrate how her dreams responded to her interest in finding out about her relationship to Christ and Life. Most of the reincarnation references are generalized to lend support to her conscious interest in this subject as an explanation of the evolution of the soul. Since the dream is so long I have chosen to interrupt it with interpretive comments.

> *I think I lost the beginning* (we've all lost our beginning and that is why we are on our earth journey!) *I also lost the answer as to what was the project we were on and why.*
>
> *I dreamed I was working on some kind of project that involved the A.R.E.* (This shows the area of her life that the dream is concerned with. Her A.R.E. project is HER search for God!)
>
> *Chris was in it.* (This Chris was a member of her study group whose name was really Christ. I think the Christ of the study group stood for his namesake—Jesus Christ and for the Christ within the dreamer and in all of us. Therefore, Christ is involved in her search for God!) *In fact quite a few people were working though I didn't recognize anyone else.* (She's not alone in searching for God!). *I was walking to Christ's house* (house is usually a symbol for consciousness, she is walking toward Christ Consciousness). *The house was on a corner* (turning point or crossroads). *It wasn't until I turned right* (she's made the correct turn by starting her search for God!) *and faced the front of the house* (she's facing, studying, the example of Christ's life) *that I realized I had passed this house in another dream* (she's worked on this in previous lives).

Christ's grandson (Jesus Christ was a grand, that is marvelous, son of God. The Christ child in each of us is a grand son of God). *The grandson was playing in the front yard* (out in front of her consciousness she is now taking notice of this aspect) *in a sandbox* (on the earth plane!). *It was full of toys* (earth's distractions, but we learn lessons from them too, 'Play is the work of children!'). *He was a beautiful child* (our inner Christ beauty) *with dark brown curly hair and big brown eyes. The front yard was enclosed in chain-link fencing* (many lives linked in a series, reincarnation).

While we worked we all helped take care of him. (That's what we're here for!) *In the house* (in consciousness) *we seemed to be clearing up* (Good for her!) *and shelving books* (many lives — reincarnations) *to get ready for something* (to get back to our heavenly father).

As you looked out of the front of the house you could see what I would describe as a volcano (eternal fire at the core of the earth = eternal fire at our core, God) *in the middle of a housing tract.* (God's eternal flame is at the center of *all* individual manifestations of consciousness, we are each a spark flying off from the central flame). *It was built like an artichoke* (having a heart) *only it was made of metal* (the strength of the earth plane).

While working we heard what sounded like an explosion and ran to the front of the house to see what it was. The volcano had erupted and one of the metal leaves had blown away (in a mighty upheaval one leaf was split off—birth!). *It, the volcano, was now fiery red and it gave everything around it a red glow* (this could symbolize the birth of Jesus Christ and also how our births and lives need the glow from the central fire, God). *The piece that exploded off fell some streets* (lifetimes) *behind us on El Centro Street* (the life of Jesus Christ is some lifetimes behind us. His life was a major part of God's life and lit up the world for us. Christ is at the center of our search for God!). *I heard someone who lived on that street say they were moving away because of danger.* (Many people then and now reject Jesus because of fear.) *I felt that we weren't in any danger at all.* (She is not afraid!)

We had done as much as we could that day and were getting ready to leave when I noticed a box on the floor (her foundation?). *It looked to me like it had in it flower bulbs* (continual reblooming of life every year—her foundation of many lives). *I asked what was to be done with them. I was told they were to be planted the next day. Chris asked if I would like to see something interesting?* (the Christ consciousness within her is going to show her something interesting). *He took out one of the bulbs and cut the tip off, put it in the kitchen sink* (water of everyday life) *and it began to spread and look like an artichoke with the tip cut off.* (In the image and likeness of God!) *A puff of smoke* (cloudy atmosphere seen dimly, smoke screen) *came out of the center and I asked what it was. He said that when it hit you and you smelled it, it took you back in time* (lead in to a literal personal past-life recall!)

As he said this I found myself in a canoe with Chris and another man. (She and her Christ seed in a previous life as a man. The canoe was a vehicle for moving through life in former times as a car is nowadays). *I knew the change was instant but I also knew in that instant that we were going to die* (have to die out of this life to get back to a previous life). *We were in a stream entering a large lake* (stream—the water of one life; lake—the collected reservoir of the water/spirit/essence of many lives). *As we entered the lake I saw that it had many kinds of snakes.* (Snake is a common symbol of eternal life and reincarnation because snakes shed many skins, molt. Remember the ancient symbol of the snake in a circle biting its tail? The end is also a new beginning! In her spiritual reservoir, the lake, she has many kinds of lives.) *The ones I remember most were kind of reddish and in bunches all tangled up* (all of her past lives, karma, aren't straightened out yet). *I thought, I wouldn't want to be in that water!* (It is well that we don't remember all about our past until we do have most of it worked out!)

As we neared the other side of the lake we found that the canoe was taking in

*water and we were sinking. I was hoping
we could make it to shore in time. We were
sinking very fast, the back of the canoe
going down faster than the front where I
was. There was another canoe not far from
us and they shouted to try and help us. We
reached them but the back part sank into
the water as the people in the other canoe
helped me into theirs. I heard one of them
say that a snake had gotten the man who
had been with me in the sunken canoe.*
(Her previous life as a man was sinking
back into her reservoir.) *I don't remember
how we were dressed but the men who
picked me up were dressed like fur trappers.* (Probably that was her occupation in
that previous life as a man. Trappers
would travel through much of their life
in a canoe.) *We then shifted back to the
house.* (Back to this lifetime.)

We were working on a huge shower
(water from above heavenly, spiritual
water, her search for God project). *I was
quite excited about working on the shower
and couldn't wait to finish and take a
shower. It was a strange shower because it
was so enormous and quite high* (the spiritual waters are enormous and high!). *The
room in which the shower was being installed was about the size of a high school
gym.* (Her search for God is higher learning on the physical education plane.)

*I went to use the shower but there seemed
to be some dissension* (some reticence) *about
me using it. I went ahead and used it anyway. It was great! It felt like rainfall* (water

*from heaven, promotes growth, cleanses
the earth). It was very soothing. When I
finished I felt as if I had been energized!*

She had been energized. That was a refreshing and
invigorating dream. The dream seemed to affirm her
interest in reincarnation in a general way but not in
regard to any specific problem.

This next situation is very important to me as an
outside observer. It taught me a lot. When I first met
Mrs. Evans, she was a busy mother of three with an
interest in dream study. She had this moving story to
tell about her youngest daughter and an important
dream she had experienced.

About five years before, she had lost a three-year-old
daughter due to leukemia. Her first reaction was to be
angry at God for taking away her lovely child. She kept
muttering, "Why me, why me?" Then she had this
dream.

My two remaining older children, my
husband and I were in old fashioned peasant clothes like in the 1800's. We were
walking across a bleak land (reminded me
of the Russian Steppes). The father-hus-
band, was leading a horsedrawn hearse.
Our dead daughter was propped upright
in the hearse. I was very grieved and tor-
mented and angry. I couldn't bear to look
at my daughter's body. There was some
kind of mark on her forehead. We entered
a town and the people began to shout at us
to get out and they were throwing stones at
us. I knew it had something to do with the

> diseased way my daughter had died. I
> hated the people, I swore at them and
> shouted how I hated them and hated God,
> too.

After that dream, Mrs. Evans said she thought a lot
and concluded that it was a glimpse of a past life. Once
before she had lost a daughter and become bitter about
it. Now God was giving her another chance to accept
his judgments. A chance to realize that the Lord giveth
and the Lord taketh away. After that realization, she
lost her bitterness and took up the tasks of living again.
Then she had this dream:

> I'm in a house with many dark rooms. I
> walk down a dark hallway toward a door.
> The door is half wood and half screen. I
> look out through the screen (the veil be-
> tween this life and the life beyond). There
> is bright sunshine outside. I see my dead
> daughter alive and healthy, and with her
> hair. She is floating and flying around a
> tree. She sees me and looks sheepish, as if
> I'd caught her sneaking in a cookie jar.
> Then she disappeared.

Mrs. Evans reported feeling great release after those
two dreams. Then she had a period of creativity where
she would sit down at odd moments and write poetry.
The last poem that she wrote was:

> Your tears, your tears
> Call me back
> I will return

My eyes will be blue
My hair will be brown
I'm coming down.

Later she realized that poem was dated when she was two weeks pregnant with her now youngest daughter. This new child closely resembles the daughter who died of leukemia and the collick is the same. She feels this is her same daughter reborn to her because this time she was able to accept God's will.

This next dream requires a little background. Esther is a teacher serving black children in a ghetto school. She is Jewish. Her roommate, Joan, is also a teacher who works with minority children in another ghetto school. Their roommating relationship is rather difficult. Joan had this dream:

> I, Joan, am standing beside an ancient road in a group of ruling families of this ancient city. Everyone is dressed in ancient costumes (which she identified as Aztec Indian). Down the road comes a group of newly enslaved people.
>
> I see Esther enchained in metal armbands being jostled along in the crowd. Our eyes meet in recognition.
>
> I, Joan, feel or sense another similar scene of Nazis as leading Jews to a concentration camp.
>
> Now I see one of my fellow teachers of the present day standing beside me. This teacher's name is GRACE PRIEST.

Whether we choose to regard this as a literal past life recall or not, it bears an important message for both girls at the present time. Does Esther feel that Joan has been "lording" it over her? Both girls, working in such difficult areas of teaching, must have a deep commitment to equalizing the unfairness of class distinction, and racial discrimination. Why? Could the dream help explain that? They thought so. Having been rulers and slaves, they know the horrors of such things and are doing what they can this time to right them.

This may be a beautiful example of the law of cause and effect working out. Karma is being met and fulfilled. The glorious promise in the dream is GRACE PRIEST. Beside the dreamer is the state of Grace. When we are given Grace we are no longer subject to the law of karma. Is not the function of a Priest to serve? Grace Priest is the keynote of the whole dream. The dreamer's life of service to minority children is helping wipe out that old karma.

When I began to attend a new church and met some very inspiring people, I had this dream. Maybe it explains why I felt so comfortable with them, had we perhaps been together in former lives?

> My school principal (boss, higher mind) came to my office. He was getting some books from my shelf to give to some parents (older people) who had come to school to help (a helpful group). He selected the old edition of a book titled "Our New Friends." He could have taken copies of the new edition which were beside the old ones on

> the shelf. He insisted on taking the old
> edition.

I felt it meaningful to consider that as a message. It tells me that my new friends are familiar to me because I've known them in their old editions. Thank you, Ben Franklin, for that bit of symbolism.

Mark was fascinated by the idea of reincarnation and really wanted to know what famous person he had been before. Please note there was not one famous person in any of these dream examples—only meaningful insights. Mark kept asking his dream mind to give him a past life recall just because he was curious about it. His dream answer was helpful but not what he expected.

> I got into my car, tried to look back, but
> there was NO REAR VIEW MIRROR!

At another point in my philosophical and spiritual search, I became acquainted with another occult group. While still wondering about their ideas, I had this dream. It is so-o-o funny, but it says exactly what it intended to say.

> I'm in a large auditorium (audio indi-
> cates hear this). Various people from 'The
> Group' are milling around not doing any-
> thing in particular (not a productive
> group). I look down and notice I am bare
> breasted and my contact lenses are on the
> ends of my boobs!

I woke up thinking that was really strange. Since the people from 'The Group' were the only other feature of the dream, I knew that was what the dream was about. Suddenly it came to me. Now I can see through these boobs! My delighted laughter woke up my husband. But that was a good bit of spiritual guidance. I don't think a group of non-productive boobs is likely to lead me to heaven.

Chapter 9

Biblical Precedents for Practical Guidance From Dreams

For God speaketh once, yea twice, yet
man perceiveth it not. In a dream, in a
vision of the night, when deep sleep
falleth upon men, in slumberings upon the
bed; Then he openeth the ears of men, and
sealeth their instruction, That he may
withdraw man from his purpose, and hide
pride from man.

Job 33:14-17

It occurred to me that most non-fiction books have a section about the history of their topic. Also, this approach to dreams might have more credence for some people if I showed some precedence for it. So this chapter contains examples of dreams from the Bible, organized and looked at from the point of view of the chapters in this book. I used the Scofield Bible as my reference.

First, a health and diet dream of practical guidance for an entire nation! It could also be considered as occupational guidance for the dreamer since a Pharaoh's job is the welfare of his people.

> "And it came to pass at the end of two full years, that Pharaoh dreamed: and behold, he stood by the river Nile (symbolic of Egyptian nation).
>
> And, behold, there came up out of the river (nation) seven well favored kine (cattle) and fat fleshed; and they fed in a meadow (symbolic of a nation's meat production).
>
> And, behold, seven other kine came up after them out of the river, ill favored and lean fleshed (poor national meat production); and stood by the other kine upon the brink of the river. And the ill favored and lean fleshed kine did eat up the seven well favored and fat kine. So Pharaoh awoke.
>
> And he slept and dreamed the second time: and behold, seven ears of corn (symbolic of agricultural production) came up upon one stalk, rank and good. And, behold, seven thin ears (poor agricultural production) and blasted with the east wind (symbolic of the drought) sprung up after them. And the seven thin ears devoured the seven rank and full ears. And Pharaoh awoke, and, behold, it was a dream."
>
> Genesis 41:1–7

"And Joseph said unto Pharaoh, the dream of Pharaoh is one: God hath shewed Pharaoh what he is about to do. The seven good kine are seven years; and the seven good ears are seven years; the dream is one. And the seven thin and ill favoured kine that came up after them are seven years; and the seven empty ears blasted with the east wind shall be seven years of famine. This is the thing which I have spoken unto Pharaoh: What God is about to do he sheweth unto Pharaoh.

"Behold, there come seven years of great plenty throughout all the land of Egypt: And there shall arise after them seven years of famine; and all the plenty shall be forgotten in the land of Egypt; and the famine shall consume the land; And the plenty shall not be known in the land by reason of the famine following; for it shall be very grievous. And for that the dream was doubled unto Pharaoh twice; it is because the thing is established by God, and God will shortly bring it to pass."   Genesis 41:25-32

Also in the category of physical or health guidance could come dreams of warning — life-saving dreams.

Concerning the wise men from the east who came to worship the birth of Christ.

"He (Herod) sent them to Bethlehem, and said, Go and search diligently for the young child; and when ye have found him, bring me word again, that I may come and worship him also."   Matthew 2:8

> "And being warned of God in a dream
> that they should not return to Herod, they
> departed into their own country another
> way."   Matthew 2:12

Also, Joseph, whose job it was to care for his family had a warning dream.

> "And when they were departed, behold,
> the angel of the Lord appeareth to Joseph

in a dream, saying, Arise, and take the
young child and his mother, and flee into
Egypt, and be thou there until I bring thee
word: for Herod will seek the young child
to destroy him."   Matthew 2:13

Now, I'm going to bring together some dreams I call
destiny dreams. Three promise survival and therefore
would give the dreamer peace of mind in the face of
danger; psychological support for greater mental health.

First of all, Joseph as a young man. His destiny dream
came when he would be rightfully upset because his
older brothers hated him. "And when his brethren saw
that their father loved him more than all his brethren,
they hated him and could not speak peaceably unto
him."   Genesis 37:4

"And Joseph dreamed a dream and he
told it to his brethren . . . For, behold, we
were binding sheaves in the field, and lo,
my sheaf arose, and also stood upright;
and behold your sheaves stood round about,
and made obeisance to my sheaf.

And his brethren said to him, Shalt thou indeed
reign over us? or shalt thou indeed have dominion over
us? And they hated him yet the more for his dreams,
and for his words.

And he dreamed yet another dream and told it . . .

Behold, the sun and the moon and the
eleven stars made obeisance to me.

And he told it to his father, and to his brethren; and
his father rebuked him and said unto him, 'What is

this dream that thou hast dreamed? Shall I and thy mother and thy brethren indeed come to bow down ourselves to thee to the earth?" Genesis 37:9-10

Two other destiny dreams; one bringing hope, the other preparing the dreamer for death.

"And Pharaoh was wroth against two of his officers, against the chief of the butlers, and against the chief of the bakers. And he put them inward in the house of the captain of the guard, into the prison . . . And they dreamed a dream both of them, each man his dream in one night . . .

> And the chief butler told his dream to Joseph, and said to him, In my dream, behold, a vine was before me: And in the vine were three branches; and it was as though it budded, and her blossoms shot forth; and the clusters thereof brought forth ripe grapes: And Pharaoh's cup was in my hand: and I took the grapes, and pressed them into Pharaoh's cup, and I gave the cup into Pharaoh's hand.

And Joseph said unto him, "This is the interpretation of it; The three branches are three days: Yet within three days shall Pharaoh lift up thine head and restore thee unto thy place and thou shalt deliver Pharaoh's cup into his hand, after the former manner when thou wast his butler." Genesis 40:2-13

> When the chief baker saw that the interpretation was good, he said unto Joseph, I also was in my dream, and, behold, I had three white baskets on my head. And in the

> uppermost basket there was of all manner of bakemeats for Pharaoh: and the birds did eat them out of the basket upon my head.

And Joseph answered and said, "This is the interpretation thereof: The three baskets are three days: Yet within three days shall Pharaoh lift up the head from off thee, and shall hang thee on a tree; and the birds shall eat thy flesh from off thee."   Genesis 40:16-19

Later the butler tells Pharaoh, "And it came to pass, as he interpreted to us, so it was; me ye restored unto mine office, and him (the baker) ye hanged."

In the New Testament when Paul is being taken by ship to Rome, he has a destiny dream concerning the crew of the ship which is caught in a terrible storm.

"And when neither sun nor stars in many days appeared, and no small tempest lay on us, all hope that we should be saved was then taken away. But after long abstinence Paul stood forth in the midst of them, and said . . . 'I exhort you to be of good cheer: for there shall be no loss of any man's life among you, but of the ship.

> For there stood by me this night the angel of God, whose I am, and whom I serve, saying, Fear not, Paul; thou must be brought before Caesar: and lo, God hath given thee all them that sail with thee.
>
> Wherefore, sirs, be of good cheer: for I believe God, that it shall be even as it was told to me. Howbeit we must be cast upon a certain island.'   Acts 27:20-26

"And falling into a place where two seas met, they ran the ship aground; and the forepart stuck fast, and remained unmoveable, but the hinder part was broken with the violence of the waves . . . they which could swim should cast themselves first into the sea, and get to land; And the rest, some on boards, and some on broken pieces of the ship. And so it came to pass, that they escaped all safe to land."   Acts 27:41-4

Would you believe there is even a dream series in the Bible which shows financial guidance? Jacob had been sent by his father to get a wife from his Uncle Laban. First he served seven years for Rachel and was tricked by Laban and got Leah instead. Then Jacob served Laban another seven years to get Rachel. Then he made a deal with Laban to get all the cattle which were ring-straked, speckled and grisled. This turned out to be a lot of cattle and Laban and his sons didn't want Jacob to take them. Jacob then had a dream which he told to his wives, Leah and Rachel.

> "And it came to pass at the time that the cattle conceived, that I lifted up mine eyes, and saw in a dream, and behold, the rams which leaped upon the cattle were ring-straked, speckled and grisled.
> "And the angel of God spake unto me in a dream, saying, 'Jacob': and I said, 'Here am I.' And he said, Lift up now thine eyes and see, all the rams which leap upon the cattle are ring-straked, speckled and grisled: for I have seen all that Laban doeth unto thee.

"I am the God of Beth-el, where thou anointedst the pillar, and where thou vowedst a vow unto me: now arise, get thee out from this land, and return unto the land of thy kindred." Genesis 31:10-13

"Then Jacob rose up, and set his sons and his wives upon camels; And he carried away all his cattle and all his goods which he had gotten, the cattle of his getting . . . for to go to Isaac his father in the land of Canaan." Genesis 31:17-18

"And it was told Laban on the third day that Jacob was fled. And he took his brethren with him and pursued after him seven days' journey . . .

And God came to Laban the Syrian in a dream by night, and said unto him, "Take heed that thou speak not to Jacob either good or bad." Genesis 31:22-25

This was part of their conversation Jacob speaks: "Thus have I been twenty years in thy house; I served thee fourteen years for thy two daughters, and six years for thy cattle: and thou hast changed my wages ten times. Except the God of my father, the God of Abraham, and the fear of Isaac, had been with me, surely thou hadst sent me away now empty. God hath seen mine affliction and the labour of my hands, and rebuked thee yesternight." Genesis 31:41-42

So, I would consider Laban's dream one of personal growth and character development, while Jacob's was for his financial help.

King Nebuchadnezzar's dream foretelling his madness could be a dream of guidance for personal growth and mental health. He had the dream a year before his madness, but he did not change his ways, he did not heed the message of the dream. Therefore, his pride, and ego inflation, led to a seven year siege of madness while the instinctual side of his psyche took over to restore balance with the exaggerated ego.

"I, Nebuchadnezzar, was at rest in mine house, and flourishing in my palace: I saw a dream which made me afraid, and the thoughts upon my bed and the visions of head troubled me." Daniel 4:4-5

"Thus were the visions of mine head in my bed; I saw, and behold a tree in the midst of the earth, and the height thereof was great. The tree grew and was strong, and the height thereof reached unto heaven, and the sight thereof to the end of all the earth: The leaves thereof were fair, and the fruit thereof much, and in it was meat for all: the beasts of the field had shadow under it and the fowls of heaven dwelt in the boughs thereof, and all flesh was fed of it. I saw in the visions of my head upon my bed, and behold, a watcher and an holy one came down from heaven: He cried aloud, and said thus, Hew down the tree, and cut off his branches, shake off his leaves, and scatter his fruit: let the beasts get away from under it, and the fowls from his branches: Nevertheless leave the stump of his roots in the earth, even with a band of iron and brass, in the tender grass of the field; and let it be wet with the dew of heaven, and let his portion be with the beasts in the grass of the earth:

Let his heart be changed from man's,
and let a beast's heart be given unto him;
and let seven times pass over him. This
matter is by decree of the watchers, and
the demand by the word of the holy ones:
to the intent that the living may know that
the most High ruleth in the kingdom of
men, and giveth it to whomsoever he will
and setteth up over it the basest of men.

This dream I King Nebuchadnezzar
have seen."   Daniel 4:10-18

The summary of Daniel's interpretation is: "It is
thou O king that are grown and become strong: for thy
greatness is grown and reacheth unto heaven, and thy
dominion to the end of the earth."   Daniel 4:22

"That they shall drive thee from men, and thy dwell-
ing shall be with the beasts of the field, and they shall
make thee to eat grass as oxen, and they shall wet thee
with the dew of heaven, and seven times shall pass over
thee, till thou know that the most High ruleth in the
kingdom of men . . . And whereas they commanded
to leave the stump of the tree roots; thy kingdom shall
be sure unto thee, after that thou shalt have known
that the heavens do rule." (Daniel now urges Nebuchadnezzar to use this dream lesson for personal growth.)

"Wherefore, O, king, let my counsel be acceptable
unto thee, and break off thy sins by righteousness and
thine iniquities by shewing mercy to the poor; if it may
be a lengthening of thy tranquility."   Daniel 4:25-27

But he ignored the dream lesson and later went
temporarily crazy. "And he was driven from men and
did eat grass as oxen and his body was wet with the dew

of heaven, till his hairs were grown like eagles' feathers, and his nails like birds' claws. And at the end of the days, I, Nebuchadnezzar lifted up mine eyes unto heaven, and mine understanding returned unto me."

Daniel 4:33-34

"At the same time my reason returned unto me and for the glory of my kingdom, mine honour and brightness returned to me . . . and excellent majesty was added unto me. Now I, Nebuchadnezzar, praise and extol and honour the King of heaven . . . those that walk in pride he is able to abase."   Daniel 4:36-37

While we're on the subject of personal growth and character development through dreams, let's look at Solomon's dream.

> "In Gibeon the Lord appeared to Solomon in a dream by night: and God said, 'Ask what I shall give thee.' And Solomon said, 'Thou hast shewed unto thy servant David my father great mercy, according as he walked before thee in truth, and in righteousness, and in uprightness of heart with thee; and thou hast kept for him this great kindness, that thou hast given him a son to sit on his throne, as it is this day. And now, O Lord my God, thou hast made thy servant king instead of David my father; and I am but a little child: I know not how to go out or come in. And thy servant is in the midst of thy people which thou hast chosen a great people, that cannot be numbered nor counted for multitude.
>
> Give therefore thy servant an understanding heart to judge thy people, that

I may discern between good and bad: for who is able to judge this thy so great a people?' And the speech pleased the Lord that Solomon had asked this thing. And God said unto him, 'Because thou hast asked this thing, and hast not asked for thyself long life; neither hast asked riches for thyself, nor hast asked for the life of thine enemies; but hast asked for thyself understanding to discern judgment; Behold, I have done according to thy words: lo, I have given thee a wise and an understanding heart; so that there was none like thee before thee, neither after thee shall any arise like unto thee. And I have also given thee that which thou hast not asked, both riches, and honour; so that there shall not be any among the kings like unto thee all thy days. (Now it becomes also a spiritual guidance dream.)

And if thou wilt walk in my ways, to keep my statutes and my commandments, as thy father David did walk, then I will lengthen thy days.

And Solomon awoke and, behold, it was a dream."

I Kings 3:5-15

Another Biblical dream of spiritual guidance came to Jacob while he was enroute to Laban to seek a wife. "And he lighted upon a certain place, and tarried there all night, because the sun was set; and he took of the stone of that place, and put them for his pillows, and lay down in that place to sleep. And he dreamed:

And behold a ladder set up on the earth, and the top of it reached to heaven: and behold the angels of God ascending and descending on it. And behold, the Lord stood above it and said, 'I am the Lord God of Abraham thy father and the God of Isaac: the land whereupon thou liest, to thee will I give it, and to thy seed; (real-estate guidance? Jacob did come back to this place).

And thy seed shall be as the dust of the earth, and thou shalt spread abroad to the west, and to the east, and to the north, and to the south: and in thee and in thy seed shall all the families of the earth be blessed' (destiny dream he became the father of twelve children, the leaders of the twelve tribes of Israel).

And, behold, I am with thee, and will keep thee in all places whither thou goest, and will bring thee again into this land; for I will not leave thee, until I have done that which I have spoken to thee of.

And Jacob awaked out of his sleep, and he said, 'Surely the Lord is in this place; and I knew it not . . ! And Jacob vowed a vow, saying 'If God will be with me, and will keep me in this way that I go, and will give me bread to eat, and raiment to put on, So that I come again to my father's house in peace; then shall the Lord be my God.'" Genesis 28:11–21

This dream so impressed Jacob that he vowed to be a worshipper of the God (religion) of his fathers (nationality). He would try to be a religious and spiritual minded man.

Now let's look at dreams with occupational guidance that appear in the Bible. First and most unusual is

Daniel's experience. King Nebuchadnezzar had dreamed a dream and it really impressed him but he couldn't remember it! So he asked the Chaldean magicians, astrologers and sorcerers to show him the dream and its meaning. When none of them could help unless he could tell them the dream, he ordered all the wise men in the nation to be slain. Daniel was considered a wise man of the captives of Judah and was to be slain. Daniel and his companions prayed for help.

"That they would desire mercies of the God of heaven concerning this secret; that Daniel and his fellows should not perish with the rest of the wise men of Babylon. Then was the secret revealed unto Daniel in a *night vision*" (means dream).   Daniel 2:18-19

So he went in to King Nebuchadnezzar and said, "Thy dream, and the visions of thy head upon thy bed, are these; As for thee O king, thy thoughts came into thy mind upon thy bed, what should come to pass hereafter: and he that revealeth the secrets maketh known to thee what shall come to pass."   Daniel 2:29-30

"This image's head was of fine gold, his breast and arms of silver, his belly and his thighs of brass, His legs of iron, his feet part of iron and part of clay. Thou sawest till that a stone was cut out without hands, which smote the image upon his feet that were of iron and clay, and brake them to pieces. Then was the iron, the clay, the brass, the silver, and the gold, broken to pieces together, and became like the chaff of the summer threshing floors; and the wind carried them away, that no place was

> found for them: and the stone that smote
> the images became a great mountain, and
> filled the whole earth.

This is the dream; and we will tell the interpretation thereof before the king. Thou, O king, art a king of kings: for the God of heaven hath given thee a kingdom, power, and strength, and glory . . . Thou art this head of gold. And after thee shall arise another kingdom inferior to thee and another third kingdom of brass," etc. . . .   Daniel 2:32–39

"Forasmuch as thou sawest that the stone was cut out of the mountain without hands, and that it brake in pieces the iron and brass, the clay, the silver, and the gold; the great God hath made known to the king what shall come to pass hereafter."   Daniel 2:45

We will bypass the long range political prophecy interpretation of this dream. On the level of King Nebuchadnezzar's personal life, it looks like another dream similar to the dream about the tree which was hewed down. His kingdom will be toppled to teach him a lesson in humility. But the point right now is how Daniel's dreaming of the king's forgotten dream helped him in his job as wise man.

"Then the king Nebuchadnezzar fell upon his face, and worshipped Daniel, and commanded that they should offer an oblation and sweet ordours unto him."   Daniel 2:46

"Then the king made Daniel a great man, and gave him many great gifts, and made him ruler over the whole province of Babylon, and chief of the governors over all the wise men of Babylon."   Daniel 2:48

Edgar Cayce was also able in his trance state to trace back and find what other people had dreamed and forgotten or weren't remembering correctly!

There is another dream giving occupational guidance which is recorded in the Bible. It concerns Gideon, a miller who had become a soldier. Judges 6:11 establishes that Gideon has been a miller. "And there came an angel of the Lord, and sat under an oak which was in Ophrah that pertained unto Joash the Abi-ezrite: and his son Gideon threshed wheat by the winepress, to hide it from the Midianites." Judges 6:11

Later Gideon had three hundred men to lead against a host of Midianites. While they waited for the battle one of Gideon's men had a dream.

> "And when Gideon was come, behold, there was a man that told a dream unto his fellow, and said, "Behold I dreamed a dream, and lo, a cake of barley bread (symbol of Gideon, a miller) tumbled into the host of Midian, and came unto a tent, and smote it that it fell, and overturned it, that the tent lay along.

"And his fellow answered and said, This is nothing else save the sword of Gideon the son of Joash, a man of Israel: for into his hand hath God delivered Midian and all the host. And it was so, when Gideon heard the telling of the dream and the interpretation thereof, that he worshipped, and returned into the host of Israel and said, Arise; for the Lord hath delivered into your hand the host of Midian." Judges 7:13-15

They won the battle!

Wives can dream advice for husbands concerning their jobs. For example, we have the report of Pilate's wife and his part, as governor, in the fate of Jesus.

"When he was set down on the judgment seat, his wife said unto him saying, Have thou nothing to do with that just man: for I have suffered many things this day in a dream because of him."   Matthew 27:19

"When Pilate saw that he could prevail nothing, but that rather a tumult was made, he took water, and washed his hands before the multitude, saying, I am innocent of the blood of this just person: see ye to it. Then answered all the people, and said, His blood be on us and on our children."   Matthew 27:24-25

There is one more practical area of living that has dream guidance represented in the Bible. That is interpersonal relationships.

"And Abraham journeyed from thence toward the south country, and dwelled between Kadesh and Shur, and sojourned in Gerar. And Abraham said of Sarah his wife, She is my sister: and Abimelech king of Gerar sent, and took Sarah.

> But God came to Abimelech in a dream by night, and said to him, Behold, thou art but a dead man, for the woman which thou hast taken; for she is a man's wife. But Abimelech had not come near her: and he said, Lord wilt thou slay also a righteous nation? Said he not to me, She is my sister? and she, even she herself said, He is my brother: in the integrity of my heart and innocency of my hands have I done this.

> And God said unto him in the dream,
> Yea, I know that thou didst this in the
> integrity of thy heart; for I also withheld
> thee from sinning against me: therefore
> suffered I thee not to touch her.
>
> Now therefore restore the man his wife;
> for he is a prophet, and he shall pray for
> thee, and thou shalt live: and if thou re-
> store her not, know thou that thou shalt
> surely die, thou and all that are thine."
>
> Genesis 20:1–7

And last, but not least, there was that difficult decision for Joseph prior to the birth of Jesus.

"Now the birth of Jesus Christ was on this wise: When his mother, Mary was espoused to Joseph, before they came together, she was found with child of the Holy Ghost. Then Joseph her husband, being a just man, and not willing to make her a public example, was minded to put her away privily. But while he thought on these things:

> Behold the angel of the Lord appeared
> unto him in a dream, saying, Joseph, thou
> son of David, fear not to take unto thee
> Mary thy wife: for that which is conceived
> in her is of the Holy Ghost. And she shall
> bring forth a son, and thou shalt call his
> name JESUS: for he shall save his people
> from their sins.

"Then Joseph being raised from sleep did as the angel of the Lord had bidden him, and took unto him his wife."   Matthew 1:18–26

Now that I've looked at the Biblical dreams from the aspect of practical guidance, I'm more convinced than ever. One of the main purposes of dreams is to bring us practical guidance for everyday living.

And now any readers who have made it this far, you deserve and I wish to you —

Pleasant Dreams All Ways and Always!

Bibliography

Bro, Harmon H., *Edgar Cayce on Dreams*. New York, Paperback Library Books, 1968.

Crisp, Tony, *Do You Dream?*. New York, E.P. Dutton & Co., 1972.

DeBecker, Raymond, *The Understanding of Dreams*. New York, Hawthorn Books, Inc., 1962.

Faraday, Ann, Ph.D., *Dream Power*. New York, Berkley Medallion Books, 1973.

Faraday, Ann, Ph.D., *The Dream Game*. New York, Harper & Row Publishers, 1974.

Garfield, Patricia, Ph.D., *Creative Dreaming*. New York, Simon & Schuster, 1974.

Hall, Calvin and Nordby, Vernon, *The Individual and His Dreams*. New York, New American Library, Inc., 1972.

Hill, Brian, compiler, *Gates of Horn and Ivory: An Anthology of Dreams*. New York, Taplinger Publishing Co., 1968.

Mahoney, Maria F., *The Meaning in Dreams and Dreaming*. New York, Citadel Press, 1969.

Sechrist, Elsie, *Dreams Your Magic Mirror*. New York, Cowles Education Corp., 1968.

Sonnet, Andre, translated by Tony Frazer, *The Twilight Zone of Dreams*. New York, Chilton Book Co., 1961.

Ullman, Montague, M.D. and Krippner, Stanley, Ph.D. with Vaughan, Alan, *Dream Telepathy*. New York, Macmillan Publishing Co. Inc., 1973.

SUN – SUPERCONSCIOUS – GUIDANCE

MAN – SELF-CONSCIOUS – CONTROL

MOON – SUBCONSCIOUS – FORCES

*"A dream not remembered
is like a letter unopened."*

Talmud

BY THE SAME AUTHOR

Janice Baylis has also written a series of lessons and exercises to teach the average person HOW-TO interpret dreams. This HOW-TO MANUAL comes with a separate and specially designed PERSONAL DREAM JOURNAL notebook for recording and relating to your dreams.

DREAM DYNAMICS AND DECODING:
AN INTERPRETATION MANUAL

Table of Contents

Available from:

SUN, MAN, MOON, INC.   Manual: $7.95
Box 5084, Huntington Beach, CA 92646   Journal: $2.00